Origins of a Legend: The Making of Ed "Strangler" Lewis

By Ken Zimmerman Jr.

Origins of a Legend: The Making of Ed "Strangler" Lewis

Copyright 2024 by Ken Zimmerman Jr.

Published by Ken Zimmerman Jr. Enterprises www.kenzimmermanjr.com

All rights reserved. No part of this book may be reproduced, stored in a retrieval system, or transmitted in any form or by any means—electronic, mechanical, photocopy, recording, or any other—except for brief quotations in printed reviews without the prior permission of the publisher.

Published in St. Louis, Missouri by Ken Zimmerman Jr. Enterprises.

First Edition: January 2024

If you like this book, you can sign up for Ken's newsletter to receive information about future book releases. You can sign up for the newsletter and receive an added e-book at kenzimmermanjr.com.

Table of Contents

Introduction 7

Chapter 1 – First Matches 11

Chapter 2 – Taking a New Name................................ 17

Chapter 3 – William Demetral and Young Olsen 28

Chapter 4 – Early Battles with Dr. Roller 42

Chapter 5 – Wrestling for the American Heavyweight Wrestling Championship 57

Chapter 6 – Rematch with William Demetral 69

Chapter 7 – Meeting Billy Sandow 81

Chapter 8 – Still in Kentucky to Start 1914 96

Chapter 9 – Branching Out into Alabama 118

Chapter 10 – First Match in Georgia 131

Chapter 11 – Under New Management..................... 148

Chapter 12 – Revealing the New Manager 163

Chapter 13 – Working with Billy Sandow................. 173

Chapter 14 – Exploding the Myth about the Partnership 189

Chapter 15 – Trying to Stay Busy 197

Chapter 16 – Fall 1915 214

Conclusion 227

Other Combat Sports Books by Ken Zimmerman Jr. 230

Bibliography 231

About the Author 234

Endnotes 236

Introduction

While I have written extensively about Frank Gotch's wrestling career, I have written much less about Gotch's only rival for the title of greatest American professional wrestler, Ed "Strangler" Lewis. Part of the reason is that Lewis wrestled his biggest matches after 1920.

I decided to start this project because Lewis' early career from 1905 to 1915 is not as well-documented as his later career. The information that does exist is questionable at best, so his early career is fertile ground for new research.

I will take assumptions into the project, which the research will blow up along the way. I decided to list the assumptions in this chapter so the readers can see how research changes assumptions along the way.

My first assumption is that carnival wrestlers taught Lewis catch-as-catch-can wrestling before his actual professional wrestling career began. It will be difficult to prove or disprove this assumption unless Lewis talked about it to the newspapers.

Lewis wrestled contests early in his career but quickly transitioned to primarily working matches with his opponents. I based this assumption on Lewis working all his Kentucky matches in 1913.

Lewis took the name Ed "Strangler" Lewis not only as an homage to Evan "Strangler" Lewis, the original Strangler, but because Lewis could not wrestle under his real name Robert Friedrich. Bob Fredericks, an Iowa wrestler, was already wrestling in Kentucky before Lewis arrived. Promoters would not book Bob Friedrich and Bob Fredericks at the same time because the billing would confuse wrestling fans.

While Lewis already displayed exceptional wrestling skills, Lewis was not the unbeatable phenomenon he would become by the end of the 1910s. I based this assumption on the series of contest Lewis wrestled with Joe Stecher in the middle of the 1910s. Wladek Zbyszko also gave Lewis a tough time on a couple of occasions.

Before he became Ed "Strangler" Lewis, he was Robert Friedrich in tiny Nekoosa, Wisconsin. It was there in 1910 that Robert Friedrich announced his presence to the professional wrestling fans. From there the legend would grow.

Figure 1-Ed "Strangler" Lewis in 1913 while wrestling in Kentucky (Public Domain)

Chapter 1 – First Matches

Robert Friedrich made his professional wrestling debut on December 27, 1910, at Brooke's Hall in his hometown of Nekoosa, Wisconsin. Friedrich was born in Nekoosa on June 30, 1891. Most available sources credit Friedrich with starting his career at fourteen years of age in 1905.

I am not discounting this information because Friedrich could have wrestled in carnival shows for four or five years before taking part in a professional contest. I could not find any professional contests before this match.

In his first contest, Friedrich wrestled "Babe" Abel, a local wrestler from nearby Madison, Wisconsin. Friedrich needed an hour and fifty-five minutes to pin Abel for the first fall. The first fall did Abel in. Friedrich slammed Abel for the second fall in forty-nine seconds.[1] Friedrich won his first professional contest in front of his hometown crowd.

Friedrich's first match also dispels one of the myths around Friedrich changing his name to Ed "Strangler" Lewis. The legend says part of the motivation for Lewis to change his name was so his parents would not find out Friedrich was wrestling professionally.

In 1910, Nekoosa had a population of 745 people. It is preposterous to think that in such a small town his parents did not know their son was wrestling professionally. The Wood County, Wisconsin newspapers carried details of Friedrich's early contests in the local newspaper.

His parents knew Friedrich wrestled professionally. Hiding his career from his parents is a delightful story and may have come from Lewis himself. It has no basis in fact.

During March 1911, Friedrich sent his hometown newspaper a blurb about his successful tour of North Dakota and Montana. Friedrich threw Joe Bleth in a Glen Ulen, North Dakota wrestling match. Friedrich had already thrown Fred Johns, who claimed the championship of North Dakota.[ii]

Friedrich left for matches in Montana after defeating Bleth. Friedrich disappears from his local newspapers after these two accounts. Further muddying the water is the appearance of Martin "Strangler" Lewis and Young Strangler Lewis in 1911.

We know for sure Robert Friedrich was not Martin "Strangler" Lewis. Friedrich weighed about two hundred pounds. Martin Lewis, who claimed a distant relationship with Evan "Strangler" Lewis, weighed at least 230 pounds ruling out an early Friedrich alias.[iii] Young Strangler Lewis is more troublesome.

"Young Strangler" Lewis, who promoters billed from Carlisle, Pennsylvania, shows up in the Northeast in 1912. He wrestled Stanislaus Zbyszko in early 1912 resulting in Zbyszko breaking Young Strangler Lewis' ribs and fracturing Lewis' shoulder blade.[iv]

It is harder to drop Young Strangler Lewis as a young Robert Friedrich alias because the newspapers did not carry a photo or artist rendering of "Young Strangler" Lewis. The newspaper accounts also do not list Lewis' height or weight. However, we are fortunate in having one account from the *Vermont Phoenix*.

On June 25, 1912, Fritz Hanson defended his welterweight wrestling championship against Young Stranger Lewis. Hanson defeated Lewis in two straight falls. Hanson used a hammerlock to pin Young Strangler Lewis in 34 minutes for the first fall. Hanson won the second fall in 15 minutes with a shoulder lock and leg scissors.[v]

While Hanson winning in two straight falls in what appears to have been a legitimate contest tells us Young Strangler Lewis is not Bob Friedrich from

Nekoosa, Wisconsin, the title defense in the welterweight division cinches it for us.

Friedrich weighed between 190 and 200 pounds in the few accounts we have of him prior to 1913. Friedrich is a solid heavyweight, who could never get down to the 165-pound welterweight limit. I have no idea who "Young Strangler" Lewis was, but he was not Bob Friedrich.

Despite the sparse reporting on Friedrich's career, he was either wrestling actively, taking part in serious training or both. In early 1913, Friedrich appeared with a new name and introduced himself to wrestling fans as a top new contender with world championship potential.

Figure 2-Photo of Ed "Strangler" Lewis in his younger years. Newspaper photo includes his real name. (Public Domain)

Chapter 2 – Taking a New Name

Robert Friedrich took the biggest step in his young career, when he moved to Lexington, Kentucky in January 1913. Taking the name Ed "Strangler" Lewis and collaborating with promoter Jerry M. Walls, who also served as Lewis' manager, Lewis built a national reputation through matches with Dr. Benajmin F. Roller, Charlie Olson, and William Demetral.

Kentucky also supplied the impetus for Friedrich to change his name. Bob Fredericks, a French-Canadian wrestler based in Lansing, Iowa, wrestled regularly in Lexington and Louisville, Kentucky in early 1913. Walls would not want both a Bob Friedrich and Bob Fredericks wrestling on the same show.

In the finest tradition of American professional wrestling, Fredericks wrestled in Kentucky first. The impetus fell on Friedrich to change his name leading Friedrich to take a name in homage to the most famous professional wrestler from Wisconsin, Evan "The Strangler" Lewis.

In addition to the name, Ed "Strangler" Lewis also started using Evan Lewis' pet hold, the front face lock or guillotine choke in modern mixed martial arts terms.

Lewis wrestled Fredericks in his first Kentucky match in Louisville, Kentucky on January 24, 1913.[vi] The men wrestled at the Buckingham Theater on mats placed on the stage.

In this match, Walls billed Lewis from Lacrosse, Wisconsin. Fredericks agreed to allow the stranglehold in the best two-out-of-three-falls match. Fredericks stipulated that if a third fall were necessary the winner of the quickest fall would decide whether to allow the stranglehold.[vii]

Lewis and Fredericks worked an exciting match. Lewis won the first fall with the stranglehold in seventeen minutes. Fredericks won the second fall with a toehold in twenty-two minutes.

Since Lewis won the first fall five minutes quicker than Fredericks won the second, Lewis insisted that he be able to use the stranglehold in the third fall.

Figure 3-Ed "Strangler" Lewis using the stranglehold on Ivan Linow circa 1917 before Athletic Commissions banned the hold. Lewis switched to the headlock after the ban. (Public Domain)

Lewis and Fredericks added a little excitement in the third fall on purpose or by accident when they tied up near the edge of the mat. The men collided with such force that both men fell off the stage over the floodlights.[viii]

Lewis was on the bottom of the pile and appeared injured. However, Lewis recovered quickly as the men climbed back up on the stage. Lewis applied a second stranglehold for the third fall and match at the twelve-minute mark.

Lewis made a good first impression with his success against Fredericks. Lewis did not have long to celebrate as William Demetral traveled to Kentucky for a match with Lewis.

Demetral, a Greek wrestler, wrestled out of Chicago but wrestled in Kentucky often during 1913 and 1914. Demetral wrestled Lewis off and on during this time.

On January 31, 1913, Lewis wrestled Demetral for the first time at the Buckingham Theater in Louisville, Kentucky. The men wrestled on mats set up on the theater stage, a customary practice before professional wrestling transitioned to rings like boxing.

Walls billed Demetral as "The Terrible Greek." Demetral won the first fall in twenty-four minutes with a leg scissors and wristlock combination. Lewis evened the match up after twelve minutes with a stranglehold. During the front face lock, Lewis' forearm busted open Demetral's mouth.[ix]

Four minutes into the third fall, Demetral picked Lewis up off the mat and slammed Lewis to the ground. Lewis landed half on the mat and half off with his head striking the stage floor.

The collision knocked Lewis senseless, so the referee, Ed Adamson, gave Lewis two minutes to recover. Lewis' seconds carried Lewis to the corner. Lewis could not recover after the two minutes, so Adamson awarded the third fall and match to Demetral because of Lewis' concession.[x]

Lewis used the ruse of striking his head to end a match without being pinned or submitted. Frank Gotch was one of the first wrestlers to use the head striking an object and being unable to continue in his worked title loss to Fred Beell in

1906. Lewis often used this spot while working matches in his career.

On February 6, 1913, Lewis returned to Lexington, Kentucky to challenge the winner of the Bob Fredericks-William Demetral match at the Opera House in Lexington. However, Demetral did not arrive in time.

Demetral's manager claimed that Lewis' stranglehold forced two of Demetral's teeth through his check causing an infection in Demetral's mouth.

Since Demetral could not wrestle, Lewis agreed to substitute for him. It was fortunate for Walls and his partner William Barton that Lewis intended to challenge the winner. Lewis' presence allowed Walls and Barton to preserve the card.

WILLIAM DEMETRAL, THE "TERRIBLE GREEK."

Figure 4- William Demetral billed as the "Terrible Greek" in 1913 (Public Domain)

Prior to the start of the two-out-of-three-falls match between Lewis and Fredericks, Lewis said he would throw Fredericks twice within the sixty-minute time limit. Even though the match ended with both Lewis and Frederick scoring a fall, Fredericks won the match because Lewis did not throw Fredericks twice in an hour.[xi]

Walls and Lewis setup the stipulations to preserve the Demetral-Fredericks match. The 250 fans who attended the match were not disappointed with Lewis replacing Demetral as they enjoyed the match.

Lewis signed to wrestle Jack Stone from Seattle, Washington on February 19, 1913, in Lexington. Stone did not live in Seattle but Louisville, Kentucky. Walls preference for Stone led to the friction between Walls and Lewis later in their partnership.

Lewis agreed to the named promoter W.H. Barton, Walls' business partner, barring the stranglehold for the first fall. Lewis could use the stranglehold in the second fall. If a third fall were necessary, the winner of the shortest fall would decide whether to allow the stranglehold or not.[xii]

Jack Stone arrived in Lexington on Valentine's Day 1913. Stone stopped in Louisville first to defeat Bob Fredericks in two straight falls. Stone trained at the Lexington YMCA. Lewis trained at the State University gymnasium.[xiii]

Barton and Wall sold tickets on the stage for $1.00. They sold the remaining tickets for twenty-five cents, fifty cents, and seventy-five cents.[xiv]

Stone won the first fall after fifty-five minutes. Lewis won the second fall, when Stone flailed away trying to escape the stranglehold. Stone and Lewis fell off the mat with Stone striking his head on the floor.

Referee E.R. Sweetland counted Stone out and awarded Lewis the second fall. Stone could not recover during the intermission. Stone conceded the match to Lewis.

Lewis announced that since he won the match on a technicality, Lewis would split the purse with Stone fifty-fifty instead of Lewis taking the winner's purse of seventy-five percent. Lewis also accepted William Demetral's challenge for a rematch in Louisville.[xv]

Lewis started his Kentucky run strongly. William Demetral and Dr. Benjamin F. Roller helped continue this ascent to national notoriety.

Figure 5- Jack Stone, a Seattle, Washington, actually Louisville, Kentucky, professional wrestler around 1913 (Public Domain)

Chapter 3 – William Demetral and Young Olsen

Before the rematch with Demetral, Lewis wrestled lightly regarded "Doc" Domer of Chicago, Illinois. Lewis wrestled Domer in Louisville on Friday, February 21, 1913.

Lewis defeated Domer in two straight falls. It took Lewis only forty-nine minutes to take both falls.[xvi] Walls booked Domer for Lewis to score a dominant win leading into bigger matches.

In early March, Lewis accepted the position of wrestling and boxing instructor for the State University in Lexington, Kentucky.[xvii] It was not unusual in this era for professional wrestlers to coach college wrestling teams. George Tragos, famous as the trainer of Lou Thesz, coached the University of Missouri wrestling team in the 1920s.

On Thursday, March 6, 1913, Lewis wrestled the German wrestler, Harry

Faust. Faust wrestled out of Chicago, Illinois.

Wrestling Match

OPERA HOUSE

Thursday Eve., Mch. 6

ED 'STRANGLER' LEWIS

vs.

HARRY FAUST.

Contest to a finish. Two falls out of three to win. Strangle hold barred.

2 Good Preliminaries.

Time Called at 8:15.

Admission—25c, 50c and 75c.

Stage Seats $1.00.

Tickets on Sale at Graddy & Bradley.

Figure 6- Lewis vs. Faust advertisement in the Lexington Herald (Public Domain)

This match started out as a work but ended up a legitimate contest. Faust may have objected to losing to the 21-year-old Lewis. Faust may also have been stronger than he was smart. It was Lewis' first experience with a double-cross or a wrestler "going into business for themselves."

Barton and Walls brought Faust to lose to Lewis, but Faust did not show much enthusiasm for the assignment. Faust butted and fouled Lewis repeatedly during the first fall.[xviii] The fans began booing Faust after the second deliberate foul.

Lewis struck back with a palm strike once or twice but stayed focused on winning the match. Lewis pinned Faust with a half-Nelson in twenty-two minutes for the first fall.

During the intersession, Barton, the promoter of record, told his partner Jerry Walls, who filled in for the normal referee, to disqualify Faust for any more fouls.

Figure 7-Harry Faust (Public Domain)

Faust quit fouling after the hard warning. Faust realized the error of his ways as he could not beat Lewis in a legitimate contest. Lewis pinned Faust with a half-Nelson and wrist hold for the second fall and match.[xix]

Faust returned to Chicago because his relatives sent him a telegram telling Faust his wife was dangerously ill with pneumonia. Barton and Walls had no interest in booking Faust again anyway.

On Wednesday, February 12, 1913, Lewis was back in Lexington to wrestle at the Opera House. Lewis wrestled Greek wrestler Gus Chamos in this match. Both men weighed one hundred ninety-eight pounds for the match.

Lewis dispatched Chamos easily. Lewis secured a half-Nelson and crotch hold combination to take the first fall in twenty-two minutes. Lewis only needed ten minutes to win the second fall with a half-Nelson.[xx] It was the second match in a row, where the promotion banned the stranglehold.

On March 14, 1913, Lewis wrestled the brother of one of the greatest light heavyweights of that or any era, Charlie Olsen. Lewis wrestled "Young" Olsen at the Buckingham Theater in Louisville, Kentucky.

Lewis had the size and strength advantage. Olsen weighed twenty pounds less but showed greater quickness.

Lewis won the first fall at twenty-eight minutes with a bar-arm and half-Nelson. Olsen won the second fall at the thirty-eight-minute mark with an arm scissors and three-quarters Nelson.[xxi]

W.H. Barton, the face of the Lexington promotion, served as the referee for this match. After the men wrestled for seven more minutes, Barton stepped in and declared the match a draw.

Barton said the chilly conditions left both wrestlers with numb hands. Barton felt in this situation, Lewis and Olsen could wrestle for hours without scoring another fall. The fans grumbled a little bit about the decision but were happy with the match.[xxii]

Figure 8- Young Olsen, the younger brother of Light Heavyweight Wrestling Champion Charlie Olsen. The resemblance is striking (Public Domain)

On Friday, March 28, 1913, Lewis wrestled a rematch with Young Olsen in Lexington, Kentucky. The men met at the Lexington Opera House. The newspapers did not report the number of spectators but said the crowd was "the best of the season."[xxiii]

The men wrestled for fifty-five minutes before Olsen gained the first fall with a toe hold. Lewis evened the match up thirty-one minutes later with a crotch hold and body lock.[xxiv]

At the twenty-minute mark of the third fall, Olsen slipped out of Lewis' hammerlock. The force of pulling out of Lewis' hold caused Olsen to fall face first to the mat. The fall knocked Olsen unconscious.

Olsen came to or at least appeared to. Olsen told the referee he could not continue. The referee awarded the third fall and match to Lewis on Olsen's failure to continue.[xxv] It was the first reported loss of Olsen's career.

With the slowness of the news or lack of the news in some areas, wrestlers often claimed to be undefeated when they lost many times in the past. It was hard for newspaper reporters to prove or disprove these claims.

Lewis told the crowd that he did not intend to win the match that way. Looking dismayed, Lewis also said he looked forward to wrestling with other top competitors.

On Tuesday, April 8, 1913, Lewis wrestled Virginia wrestler Eddie Schultz for the heavyweight wrestling championship of the South. The match in Lexington drew another big crowd.[xxvi]

Schultz won the first fall using an arm lock and half strangle hold to pin Lewis in thirty-four minutes. Fans appeared shocked that a wrestler victimized the strangler with a stranglehold.

To start the second fall, Lewis grabbed Schultz in a choke hold after the opening bell. Lewis used the strangle hold to lower Schultz to the mat and pin Schultz in two minutes, thirty seconds.

Schultz's seconds helped Schultz back to the corner.[xxvii] It did not look like Schultz could recover but Schultz recovered enough to start the third fall.

Schultz gave Lewis a tough match in the third fall. It took Lewis twenty-five minutes to pin Schultz with a body hold and half strangle hold. Lewis was the recognized champion of the South. At least in Lexington, Kentucky for a week or two.

Schultz said he would like to wrestle Lewis again if Lewis agreed not to use the strangle hold. Schultz said he did not agree with the strangle hold even though Schultz used it in the match.[xxviii]

Lewis agreed. Promoters scheduled a rematch for April 18, 1913.

While Lewis trained for the challenge of Eddie Schultz, Lewis woke up with a cold on April 12th. Lewis picked up a bottle, which he thought was cough medicine, but after taking a drink realized it was iodine.

Lewis ran to the drug store, where the pharmacist prevented Lewis' mistake from turning fatal.[xxix] Lewis resumed his early morning run the next day.

On Thursday, April 17, 1913, Lewis wrestled the rematch with Eddie Schultz with both men agreeing not to use the strangle hold. Lewis pressed the action throughout the match.

It took Lewis one hour and fourteen minutes to pin Schultz with a hammer lock and half-Nelson. After the intermission, Lewis took ten more minutes to win with a crotch and arm hold. Lewis dominated the rematch more strongly than the first match.

Lewis did not have time to celebrate his victory. Lewis travelled to Louisville for a rematch with William Demetral.

Lewis wrestled Demetral at the Buckingham Theater, a frequent venue for wrestling in Louisville. Lewis weighed a trim two hundred pounds for the match. The reporter for the *Louisville Courier-Journal* remarked that Lewis' active schedule caused Lewis to slim down from his earlier two hundred ten pounds.[xxx]

Lewis surprised the fans but not Demetral, who was working with Lewis, when Lewis won the match in straight falls. Lewis won the first fall with the stranglehold in twenty-nine minutes. Lewis won the second fall and match with a half-Nelson and headlock in five minutes.[xxxi]

The promotion was preparing Lewis for a big-name opponent. The promotion would reveal the big name after Lewis wrestled former opponent Young Olsen.

Lewis wrestled Olsen in Lexington, Kentucky on Monday, April 28, 1913. Fans crowded into the Lexington Opera House to see Lewis win the third match in the series in two straight falls.

Lewis agreed to a ban on the stranglehold before the match. For this match, Lewis relied on the hammerlock instead. Lewis won the first fall in fifty-eight minutes, thirty seconds with a hammerlock. After an intermission, Lewis used the hammerlock again to pin Olsen in twenty-three minutes, fifteen seconds.[xxxii]

Lewis finished April 1913 strong to set up a match with a nationally known contender for Frank Gotch's World Heavyweight Wrestling Championship. The wrestler not only wrestled Frank Gotch but also trained Georg Hackenschmidt for the second Gotch-Hackenschmidt match in 1911. Was Lewis up for the challenge?

Figure 9- William Demetral circa 1913 (Public Domain)

Chapter 4 – Early Battles with Dr. Roller

Ed "Strangler" Lewis' promoter Jerry M. Walls brought in a nationally recognized wrestling star in Dr. Benjamin F. Roller to take on his budding new star.

Dr. Roller obtained his medical degree by playing professional football as Roller did not have enough money to pay for his education. After receiving his doctor of physiology, Roller practiced privately for two or three years before becoming a professional wrestler in 1906.

Walls tried to arrange a match for Monday, May 5, 1913, but Roller suffered an injury wrestling a match in Canada. Roller told Walls that he thought he could make it to Lexington by May 12th.[xxxiii]

Walls was stuck in a tricky situation because he already reserved the Lexington Opera House for May 5th. Walls wired Bob Fredericks in Chicago.

Fredericks agreed to wrestle Lewis at the Opera House on May 5th.

In addition to preparing for his match with Fredericks, Lewis umpired a local baseball game in Lexington.[xxxiv] Lewis umpired at least five baseball games during the summer of 1913. The outreach to the community no doubt helped the reputation of professional wrestling in Lexington.

On May 5, 1913, Lewis wrestled Fredericks in a controversial match because of outside interference. Walls needed to preserve Lewis' big match with Roller while rewarding Fredericks for saving Walls on short notice.

Since Fredericks took the match on short notice, Lewis dropped the first fall to Fredericks. Fredericks took the first fall in twenty-one minutes with a catch and bar hold.[xxxv]

Lewis won the second fall with a half-Nelson and body hold in thirteen minutes. It was at this point that Lexington Police Officer Doyle and

Cropper told Walls and Barton that if Fredericks or Lewis fouled any more, the officers would stop the match.[xxxvi]

Lewis and Fredericks wrestled twelve more minutes before Officers Doyle and Cropper entered the ring. The officers stopped the match because of the frequent fouls.

The referee named Yaeger initially awarded the third fall and match to Lewis because Yaeger ruled that Fredericks started and continued the fouling. Yaeger felt Lewis only retaliated after Fredericks kept fouling.[xxxvii]

After thinking about it a little longer and probably with encouragement from Walls, who was grateful to Fredericks for making the last-minute booking, Yaeger changed his mind. Yaeger declared it a draw at one fall a piece.[xxxviii] Walls announced Lewis would wrestle Dr. Benjamin Roller on Wednesday, May 14, 1913.

Between the match with Fredericks and the match with Roller, Lewis wrestled a rematch with William Demetral at Lexington's MacCauley Theater on May 9, 1913. In an odd lead-up to the big match with Roller, Demetral defeated Lewis.[xxxix]

The Lexington Herald article attributed Demetral's win to Lewis' indigestion caused by buns Lewis ate at noon. While they worked the match, Lewis was sick. Lewis vomited in his corner between falls.

Demetral won the first fall in thirty-three minutes with a half-Nelson and crotch hold. Demetral won the second fall and match in seventeen minutes with a body crotch hold.[xl] Fans seemed to forget about the result of this match with Roller vs. Lewis coming up.

Local newspapers carried Dr. Roller's inspirational story which helped build up the match. Dr. Roller started his athletic career at De Pauw University in nearby Indiana. Roller achieved his first athletic fame as a star on both the varsity football and wrestling teams. Roller then attended the

University of Pennsylvania to earn his medical degree.[xli]

Roller practice privately for a couple of years in addition to working with a Professor at the University of Seattle. In Seattle, at the Seattle Athletic Club, Roller began his professional career.

Roller quickly developed a national reputation. Roller not only wrestled Frank Gotch and Joe Stecher but was the American representative for the spring version of the 1915 New York International Wrestling Tournament.[xlii]

Roller arrived in Lexington on Wednesday morning, May 14, 1913. Later that evening, Roller walked onto the stage at the Lexington Opera House to wrestle "Strangler" Lewis.

Roller stood six feet tall and weighed two hundred ten pounds. Lewis stood an inch shorter and weighed twelve pounds less at one hundred ninety-eight pounds.[xliii]

Lewis pressed the action in the match, taking the fight to Roller. Roller made Lewis look great before catching Lewis in a double leg lock with a toe hold. Lewis gave up to the toe hold at forty-eight minutes.[xliv]

Lewis limped noticeably as he stood back to his feet. His seconds helped Lewis back to the dressing room.

After ten minutes, Lewis returned to the mat in intense pain. Roller needed less than a minute to pin Lewis with a waist lock for the second fall and match.[xlv]

Lewis said he had no excuses. Roller was the better wrestler. Dr. Roller said Lewis was the finest young wrestler that Roller had faced. Considering that a high schooler named Joe Stecher almost beat Roller, when Stecher was eighteen years old, Roller's praise of Lewis made a big impression on the wrestling fans.

Figure 10- Dr. Benjamin F. Roller in 1913 (Public Domain)

Despite the defeat, Jerry Walls kept Lewis busy. Walls booked Bob Fredericks to wrestle Lewis on Wednesday, May 21, 1913, at the Lexington Opera House a week after the Roller match.

Since Lewis and Fredericks wrestled in Lexington twice before in controversial matches, Walls booked a finish match with all holds allowed, including the stranglehold and toe hold.

Lewis won the first fall with the stranglehold in eight minutes.[xlvi] Lewis looked fresh and a sure winner.

Midway through the second fall, Lewis started vomiting. Lewis vomited four times before Fredericks pinned Lewis with toe hold at twenty-eight minutes. Lewis could not recover between falls. Fredericks pinned Lewis with a crotch hold for the third fall and match at thirty minutes.[xlvii]

Lewis told reporters that strawberries and buttermilk upset his stomach. Lewis had figured out a way to make himself vomit during matches to supply a plausible reason for losing falls to his rivals.

Walls booked a rematch for Lewis with Dr. Roller for Thursday, June 5, 1913, in Lexington. However, Jack Stone had already arrived in Lexington, so Walls and Lewis decided to give Stone a rematch before Lewis wrestled Roller again.

Lewis and Stone would wrestle at the Lexington Opera House on June 5th. The men agreed to ban both the stranglehold and toe hold.

Lewis and Stone shook hands and started wrestling at 9:06 p.m. At 11:23 p.m., referee Jerry M. Walls, the Louisville promoter, stopped the match, so both men could have a ten-minute break.[xlviii]

Walls restarted the match which went another hour with neither man gaining a fall. The fans started calling for Walls to call it a draw, which Walls did after 12:30 a.m. in the morning.[xlix]

50

With a long, inconclusive match, it is possible that Lewis and Stone were shooting. However, the fast-paced action argues against that. Walls did not want Lewis to lose another match heading into the Roller match. Walls intended to keep using Jack Stone, his fellow Louisvillian, too, so a draw served his promotional purposes.

Dr. Roller wrestled a busy schedule leading into the rematch with Lewis. Roller wrestled in California, Nevada on June 7, 1913. Roller wrestled in Parsons, Missouri on June 9, 1913. Roller traveled to Windsor, Missouri for another match on June 10, 1913. Roller then traveled to Dallas, Texas for a match on June 11, 1913.[1]

Roller wrestled his first match in Kentucky at Paris, Kentucky on June 16, 1913. Roller defeated Bob Fredericks leading into the Lewis rematch.

On Tuesday, June 17, 1913, Dr. Ben Roller wrestled Ed "Strangler" Lewis for the second time. Lewis won the coin toss to start the first fall. Lewis winning the coin toss meant Lewis could use the strangle hold in the first round, but Dr. Roller could not use the toehold.

During the second fall, Dr. Roller could use the toehold, but Lewis could not use the strangle hold. If both men won a fall, the winner of the quickest fall could use his pet hold during the third fall.[li]

Each wrestler took the offensive during the fall they could use their pet holds. Lewis pursued stranglehold after stranglehold. Lewis finally secured his pet hold forcing Roller to give up after twenty-six minutes.[lii]

Lewis wrestled defensively during the second fall and almost outlasted Roller. However, Roller secured a succession of toeholds forcing Lewis to give up after nineteen minutes.

Roller's quick victory enabled Roller to use the toehold during the third fall. However, Roller threw Lewis with a hip lock for the third fall and match.[liii]

Even though Lewis lost the match, his submission victory in the first fall led newspapers around the country to print coverage of the match. In those articles, Roller correctly predicted that Lewis would win the World Heavyweight Wrestling Championship in the future.

Walls kept Lewis busy booking Lewis for a match with frequent opponent Bob "Turtle" Fredericks in Paris, Kentucky. Walls did not run many spot shows in comparison to his regular towns of Louisville and Lexington. However, Walls did occasionally book cards in Paris, Kentucky.

Lewis won the first fall in twenty-six minutes. Fredericks fouled Lewis continuously forcing the referee to disqualify Fredericks and award the match to Lewis.[liv]

Because Walls only had a handful of regular wrestlers, Walls could not feature one wrestler like promoters in the future would. Walls used a near fifty-fifty booking style with Lewis, Demetral, Fredericks, and Stone. The wrestlers traded wins and losses until Walls could book more wrestlers from outside of Kentucky.

Lewis wrestled on the final card in Lexington before Walls shut down for the summer. On Monday, June 30, 1913, Lewis wrestled "Farmer" Jones of South Dakota. Lewis defeated Jones with a toehold and armlock.[lv] Dr. Roller defeated Jack Stone in the other main event on the two-match card.

Before the widespread use of air conditioning, wrestling promotions often shut down during the summer months. Lewis told the newspapers that he would keep himself in top condition during the hot months. Lewis wanted to wrestle Roller again in the fall.

While it was the last Lexington match, Walls promoted another Paris, Kentucky show on Tuesday, July 1, 1913.

Lewis defeated Charles Clayton in two straight falls.[lvi] After this card, Lewis went into summer training in Iowa and Wisconsin.

Figure 11- Bob "Turtle" Fredericks

Chapter 5 – Wrestling for the American Heavyweight Wrestling Championship

In September 1913, Ed "Strangler" Lewis returned to Kentucky as Jerry M. Walls started booking the fall wrestling season in Lexington and Louisville. Walls, an Indianapolis native who moved to Louisville, had spent July and August back in his hometown.

Before the spring season had ended, Walls booked Lewis into a match with William Demetral on Friday, June 12th, 1913. Lewis would wrestle Demetral in Lexington. Or so both Walls and Lewis thought.

On June 9, 1913, Demetral wired Walls a telegram from Chicago. Demetral said, "Impossible to come, have hurt leg. Please postpone for another date."

The Lexington Herald-Ledger printed Walls' reply. "You are not hurt; you are just yellow. Big coward."[lvii]

William Demetral, the Greek Demon, who is to meet Dr. B. F. Roller at the Opera House next Tuesday night in the spirited double-header wrestling match.

Figure 12- William Demetral training for Dr. Roller (Public Domain)

Walls had to book another wrestler fast, so Walls turned to another Chicago wrestler. Charles Challender, "The Mysterious Conductor," agreed to travel to Lexington and wrestle Lewis on short notice.[lviii]

Lewis arrived at the Lexington Opera House to discover "the Mysterious Conductor" also backed out of the match. Challender sent Gus Castello, "The Belgian Tiger," another Chicago wrestler, in his place.[lix]

Castello weighed two hundred twenty-eight pounds but looked about thirty pounds overweight. Lewis entered the stage area next and weighed a trim one hundred ninety-five pounds.

The frequent change of opponent affected the turnout as one of the smallest crowds left the Opera House half empty. The fans who did show up saw a rough, entertaining, if not technical, match.

Castello hobbled around like something was wrong with his feet. Lewis slipped behind Castello and took him off his feet. Castello scrambled for a toehold, but Lewis slid off the mat pulling both men to the floor.[lx]

Lewis threw Castello with a headlock takedown. Castello jumped up and charged at Lewis. Lewis reversed the charging Castello, but the momentum took both off the stage. The men landed on a chair, which splintered into a hundred pieces.

As the men climbed back onto the stage, a fan heckled Castello. Castello argued with the fan, while Lewis looked amused.

When Castello returned to the match, Lewis slammed Castello repeatedly. Castello did not like Lewis slamming him and decided to charge Lewis. Lewis side stepped and Castello plunged off the stage again.

Castello's lack of ability amused the fans and Lewis, who did not show urgency in ending the one-sided match. Finally, Lewis slammed Castello, applied a body and head hold, and pinned Castello at twenty-three minutes of the first fall.[lxi]

Castello refused to shake Lewis' hand to start the second fall. Lewis shrugged and slammed Castello to the mat.

Lewis applied a toehold but let Castello slip out of it. Lewis then applied the leg scissors on Castello and patted his backside. Castello was furious but could not do anything about it.

When Lewis finally let Castello out of the leg scissors, Castello again went to the front of the stage and yelled at the stage side fans. Lewis slammed Castello with a double bar arm and ended the farce at sixteen minutes of the second fall.[lxii] Lewis won the match in two straight falls.

Walls announced after this match that Lewis would wrestle Dr. Benjamin Roller on September 19, 1913. Lewis trained for this match at State University with the wrestling team.[lxiii]

> # WRESTLING
> ## THURSDAY NIGHT
> ### DR. B. F. ROLLER
> ### —vs—
> ### ED LEWIS
>
> The strangle and toe hold barred. Stage seats now on sale at Phoenix Hotel Cigar Stand and Lewin Cigar Co.

Figure 13-Ad for the Dr. Ben Roller vs. Ed "Strangler" Lewis American Heavyweight Championship at Lexington, Kentucky in September 1913 (Public Domain)

While Lewis trained for the match with Dr. Roller, William Demetral's manager James Marneres, posted a $500.00 side bet with the sports editor of the

Lexington Herald for a rematch between Demetral and Lewis.[lxiv]

Roller arrived in Lexington for the rematch claiming the American Heavyweight Wrestling Championship that Roller won from Charles Cutler in July 1913. Roller defended his title against Lewis in this rematch.

Frustratingly, the Kentucky newspapers did not report the crowd figures for the card but did say the crowd filled the Lexington Opera House.[lxv] The Lexington Opera House, built in 1886, still stands. It has a seating capacity of 1,000 spectators, the attendance figure for this match.

The men entered the stage area at 9 p.m. on Thursday, September 18, 1913. Lewis weighed two hundred two pounds for the rematch. Dr. Roller weighed fifteen pounds more at two hundred seventeen pounds.

Dr. Roller scored the first fall with an arm roll at twenty-one minutes. Lewis complained that he "walked into it" as he left the mat for the fifteen-minute intermission.[lxvi] Lewis wrestled more carefully after giving away the first fall.

After twenty minutes of wrestling during the second fall, Lewis picked up Dr. Roller and slammed Roller onto his right shoulder. Roller escaped injury and Lewis had to use a grapevine to keep Roller from dumping him to the mat.

After fifty-five minutes, Lewis applied the leg scissors to Roller's midsection. Roller tried to escape but had to give up to the hold. Lewis sprang up and walked back to his corner. Roller's seconds had to help Roller out of the ring.[lxvii]

During the fifteen-minute intermission, the ringside physician, Dr. David Barrow, told Dr. Roller that the leg scissors broke his tenth rib.[lxviii] Dr. Barrow told Roller that he could not continue.

The referee awarded the third fall to Lewis. Dr. Roller lost the match and

American Heavyweight Wrestling Championship to Ed "Strangler" Lewis.

Two days after Lewis' victory over Roller, Jerry Walls announced Lewis' first title defense against William Demetral for Monday, September 29, 1913. Both men put up a side bet of $500.00. Walls also made Demetral put up a $50.00 forfeit. If Demetral did not show for the match Demetral would not only lose the money, but Walls would also no longer book Demetral in Kentucky.[lxix]

The September 29th match at the Lexington Opera House proved to be a controversial match. Both men wrestled roughly to start the match. Referee Jerry Walls warned both wrestlers to stop fouling.

Demetral responded by putting Lewis in a strangle hold, which both men agreed not to use in the match. Demetral not only applied a strangle hold but refused to release it. Walls pulled Demetral off Lewis. Walls then disqualified Demetral for the first fall awarding the fall to Lewis.[lxx]

When Demetral and Lewis returned to the dressing room, the Lexington Police also went to the dressing room to talk to both men. Lt. James Eagan told the wrestlers, if they promised to stop fouling, Eagan would let the match continue.[lxxi] Local police were always concerned that boxing or wrestling matches, which got out of hand, could cause fans to riot.

Lewis responded by calling Demetral a vulgar name. Demetral said, "If that's the way Lewis feels, we had just as well stop." Lewis charged Demetral and threw a punch before the Lexington Police separated the men. The police arrested both wrestlers for disorderly conduct as Walls notified the crowd that the police stopped the match.[lxxii]

Judge Southgate held the hearing on the disorderly conduct case the following morning, September 30, 1913, in the Lexington courthouse. Demetral and Lewis apologized and shook hands. Judge Southgate fined each wrestler $15 and warned them to be professional in and out of the ring.^{lxxiii}

Whether the fight was legitimate or staged to build interest in the rematch, Demetral and Lewis were not through with each other in the ring. They would soon meet again for Lewis' American Heavyweight Wrestling Championship.

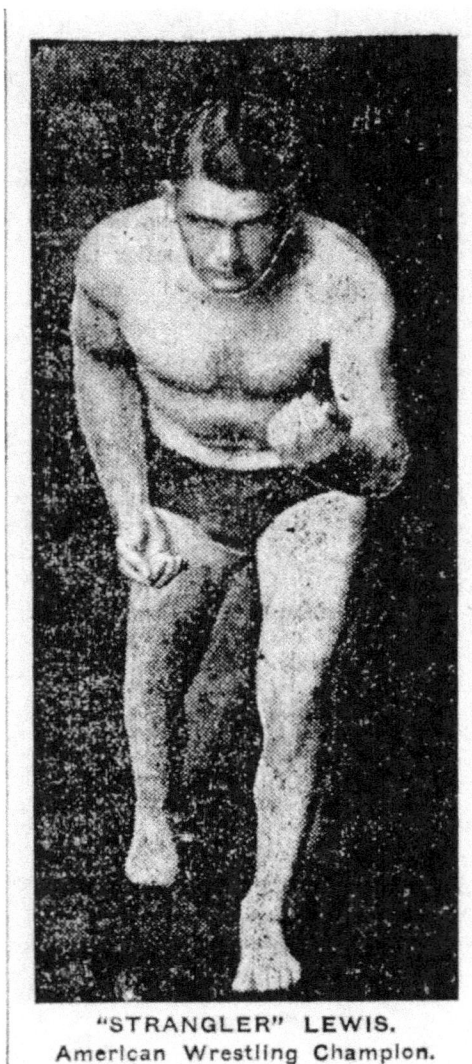

Figure 14- Ed "Strangler" Lewis at the time he won the American Heavyweight Wrestling Championship (Public Domain)

Chapter 6 – Rematch with William Demetral

Promoter Jerry Walls quickly moved to setup a rematch between Ed "Strangler" Lewis and "the Terrible Greek" William Demetral after the court case. Walls counted on the publicity from the disorderly conduct case to help sell the rematch.

Complicating Walls' desire for a quick rematch was a decision by Lexington city officials to ban professional wrestling in Lexington. However, the city officials reversed themselves less than a week later due to lobbying by Lexington's citizens.[lxxiv]

Walls could not book the Opera House but was able to book the Lexington Auditorium to host the Lewis-Demetral rematch on Tuesday, October 21, 1913. Walls told the *Lexington Herald-Leader* that Walls warned both Lewis and Demetral that any fouling would result in losing their part of the purse and Walls would ban the guilty party from wrestling in Lexington.[lxxv]

The Lexington Police also were out in force for the match to prevent a repeat of the earlier fiasco. However, both Lewis and Demetral kept this match clean.

Fans showed up for the match and supported Lewis. Lewis rewarded their support when Lewis won the first fall with a double bar lock and body hold in forty-seven minutes.[lxxvi]

The men wrestled for twenty-four minutes in the second fall, when Lewis secured a chin lock on Demetral. Demetral thrashed wildly to break the hold and accidentally pushed Lewis over the floodlights of the stage.[lxxvii]

Lewis landed heavily on his head and shoulders. Lexington Police Lieutenant Harkins quickly moved in to check on Lewis.

The referee gave Lewis fifteen minutes to recover. Three physicians were present at the match and went back to evaluate Lewis. The doctors said Lewis suffered a concussion and should not continue the match. Forced to withdraw from the match, Lewis lost the American Heavyweight Wrestling Championship to Demetral.[lxxviii]

Despite losing the title, Lewis had developed a reputation as a national level competitor. Lewis' increased fame led to other promoters booking Lewis in their towns.

Lewis accepted a booking for Macon, Georgis in November 1913. However, Walls took a more lucrative booking in Chicago, Illinois.

On Monday, November 4, 1913, Lewis wrestled Paul Martinson in a two-out-of-three-falls match. The Globe Athletic Club promoted the match at the Globe Theater in Chicago, Illinois. The promoters allowed the stranglehold in the match.[lxxix]

The Illinois newspapers incorrectly reported Lewis to be a native Kentuckian. However, Lewis or Walls could have supplied biographical information to the newspapers.

Lewis needed fifty-six minutes to secure a stranglehold on Martinson for the first fall. After a fifteen-minute intermission, Lewis secured a second stranglehold after twenty-six minutes, ten seconds to take the second fall and match.[lxxx] Lewis impressed the spectators with his first showing in Chicago.

Ed Smith, the Sporting Editor of the *Chicago American*, and long-time vocal proponent of Frank Gotch, authored an article saying the replacement for Gotch in the fan's affections may have finally arisen. Smith believed Ed "Strangler" Lewis to be authentic at only twenty-two years of age.[lxxxi]

The Globe Athletic Club booked Lewis again for Friday, November 14, 1913. Lewis hoped to wrestle Charlie Cutler but ended up booked against a giant German wrestler, Karl Schulz.

Prior to wrestling in Illinois, Lewis returned to Lexington to wrestle

Jack LeRoy of Omaha on Tuesday, November 11, 1913. Lewis defeated LeRoy in two straight falls. Lewis won the first fall with a toehold in sixteen minutes. Lewis won the second fall and match in eighteen minutes with a neck-yoke.[lxxxii]

Figure 15- Charlie Cutler (Public Domain)

Lewis returned to Chicago and wrestled Schultz, who claimed the title of wrestling champion of the German army.

Lewis and Schulz met at the Globe Theater on Friday, November 14, 1913. Lewis and Schultz were the main event of a four-match card.[lxxxiii] Four matches were a huge card in those days as cards were often only one or two matches.

Lewis made short work of Schultz. Lewis won the first fall in four minutes, forty seconds by forcing Schultz to give up to a toehold. Lewis took the second fall and match in only one minute, ten seconds with a double arm and body lock.[lxxxiv]

Lewis wrestled Paul Raas, a Swedish wrestler, a day later Saturday, November 15, 1913. Lewis wrestled Raas in front of the Chicago Athletic Association.

Lewis pinned Raas with arm scissors and wristlock combination in five minutes, ten seconds. Lewis won the match in straight falls after throwing Raas with headlock for the second fall and match in one minute, twenty seconds.[lxxxv]

Lewis winning so quickly forecast big plans for Lewis in Chicago. The promoters revealed their plans a few days later.

On Monday, November 17, 1913, Promoters Ed White and Jerry Walls accompanied by Charlie Cutler and Ed "Strangler" Lewis met in the Edelweiss restaurant to agree to terms for a match.

Cutler said the match should be winner take all. Walls said the match should be sixty percent to the winner and forty percent to the loser.

Cutler objected and said if Lewis had the guts, it should be winner take all. Lewis said, "When you wrestled Zbyszko, you didn't offer those terms did you?"

Cutler said Zbyszko was a champion, but Lewis was "yellow" or cowardly. Lewis stood up and punched Cutler, who landed on the floor and took a table with him. Lewis started to follow Cutler to the ground, but bystanders kept the men from further attacking each other.[lxxxvi] Walls announced that Lewis agreed to winner take all after the confrontation.

Wrestlers worked these angles all the time to draw interest in future matches. Lewis did punch wrestlers, when they made him angry instead of trying to cripple them with a "hook," or submission hold. They could be building up the match or Cutler made Lewis angry causing Lewis to punch Cutler for real.

The Globe Athletic Club booked the match between Lewis and Cutler for the end of the month. Lewis had one more tune-up match in Chicago prior to the big match.

On Thursday, November 20, 1913, Lewis wrestled the Mysterious Horseshoer at the Haymarket Theater. Lewis won the first fall with a bar lock and body hold in eight minutes. Lewis won the second fall and match with a half-Nelson and crotch hold in three minutes, ten seconds.[lxxxvii]

Walls also booked Lewis for a rematch with Young Olsen in Louisville, Kentucky. However, the booking violated the promotional agreement with White and

Cutler as both men agreed not to wrestle anyone else before their match in Chicago.[lxxxviii]

Ed White applied for the $250.00 deposit that both Lewis and Cutler posted to guarantee the match. White said Walls and Lewis snuck out of town to make the Louisville match. White said he might cancel Lewis' match with Cutler.

While White threatened to call off the match with Cutler, Lewis wrestled Young Olsen at the Buckingham Theater in Louisville, Kentucky. This match followed a similar pattern to Lewis' most recent matches.

Lewis won the first fall with a hammerlock in thirty minutes. Lewis won the second fall in twenty minutes with a neck-yoke that Lewis transitioned into a scissors hold and armlock.[lxxxix]

State Athletic Commissions had started banning the stranglehold. In response, Lewis started using the neck-yoke instead of the stranglehold.

On Monday, November 24, 1913, Walls and Lewis returned to Chicago. They met with Promoter Ed White and convinced White to drop the petition for the $250.00 Lewis put up to guarantee his participation in the match.

White said since Lewis emerged from Young Olsen match uninjured and ready to wrestle Cutler White would drop his request for Lewis' deposit. White confirmed that the match between Cutler and Lewis at the Globe Theater on Wednesday, November 26, 1913, was still on.[xc]

Despite all the publicity, only 1,000 fans showed up to watch the match between Lewis and Cutler.[xci] Evan "Strangler" Lewis in the 1880s drew three to six times that number of fans to his matches.

Lewis and Cutler put on a great show for the fans, who did show up. Lewis and Cutler traded holds for over an hour before Cutler took the first fall in the two-out-of-three-falls match. Cutler used a cross-body lock to pin Lewis in one hour, one minute, and thirty seconds.

Lewis appeared fresher to start the second fall. After eighteen minutes, Lewis applied his new hold, the neck-yoke, to win the second fall in eleven minutes, forty-five seconds tying the match at one fall apiece.[xcii]

Cutler came back in the third fall and applied a leg scissors, a legitimate hold, even though Cutler was working it, on Lewis' head. Cutler applied the hold convincingly as the fans yelled for the referee to stop the match. Lewis gave up at twenty-nine minutes.[xciii] Cutler won the third fall and match.

While he lost, Lewis' showing in this match continued his ascent as a rising star. However, it was a chance meeting with a manager in Kentucky, which set Lewis up for future greatness.

Figure 16- Ed "Strangler" Lewis showing his new hold, the neck-yoke, in 1913 (Public Domain)

Chapter 7 – Meeting Billy Sandow

While Ed "Strangler" Lewis wrestled Cutler in Chicago, former lightweight wrestler and now manager, Billy Sandow, arrived in Kentucky. Sandow travelled to Louisville and Lexington with the intention of booking his wrestler, Billy Jenkins, against Lewis.

Sandow started the year managing Yussuf "Young" Hussane but now managed Jenkins. Since Lewis was wrestling in Illinois, Jenkins secured a match for Jenkins with "Giant" Wallace, a Kansas wrestler reputed to the tallest professional wrestler in the United States.

Lewis planned to return to Kentucky for the holidays. Lewis had one more match to wrestle in Chicago first. On Saturday, November 20, 1913, Lewis wrestled Jack Sajatovic, a Belgian wrestler. The men wrestled at the Chicago Athletic Association Arena.

Lewis and Sajatovic wrestled for fifteen minutes before Lewis secured a vicious hammerlock. The hold injured Sajatovic, who gave up.[xciv]

Lewis appeared concerned about Sajatovic's injury and stayed away from that shoulder during the second fall. Lewis used an arm scissors on Sajatovic's good arm to take the second fall and match in two straight falls.[xcv]

On Tuesday, December 2, 1913, Lewis returned to Kentucky for the holidays. However, the Kentucky promoters forced Lewis into action as a referee.

The promoters selected Lewis to referee because both Jenkins and Wallace wanted to wrestle Lewis. The winner of the Jenkins-Wallace match would be Lewis' next challenger in Kentucky.

On Friday, December 5, 1913, Billy Jenkins, accompanied by Billy Sandow, wrestled "Giant" Wallace, accompanied by Luther Kerr. Based on looks, Wallace was an insurmountable obstacle for Jenkins.

However, looks can be deceiving in combat sports.

GIANT WALLACE.

Figure 17- Giant Wallace circa 1913 (Public Domain)

Jenkins wrestled Wallce at Jackson Hall in Lexington, Kentucky. After refereeing the Jenkins-Wallace match, "Strangler" Lewis was scheduled to wrestle an exhibition match with Tommy Devereaux to close the card out. The fans agreed Lewis refereed the Jenkins-Wallace match fairly but there was not much to the match.

Jenkins took the much larger Wallace to the mat at will. After ten minutes of wrestling, Jenkins applied a toehold and forced Wallace to give up to the painful hold.[xcvi]

Jenkins wrestled the second fall like he had a train to catch. Jenkins needed only three seconds to pin Wallace for the second fall and match. Jenkins forced Wallace to the mat with a double bar lock.[xcvii]

"Giant" Wallace represented an early version of the giant wrestler, who could not really wrestle. Promoters booked the wrestler out to different promotions, who would only use the giant once or twice because fans enjoyed the spectacle of a giant wrestler but only for a fleeting time.

After the match, Walls scheduled the match between Jenkins and Lewis for Monday, December 15, 1913, at the Lexington Opera House. The promoter, Jerry Walls, would pay the winner sixty percent of the house. Walls would pay the loser the rest of the house minus expenses.[xcviii]

At least that is what Walls told everyone. Normally, the wrestlers split the purse evenly when they worked a match.

Promoters announced these arrangements for the benefit of the athletic commissions and fans. Athletic Commissions and fans assumed the wrestlers were wrestling legitimately, or shooting, if the winner received more money than the loser.

On the night of the match, Billy Jenkins and manager Billy Sandow entered the ring first. Ed "Strangler" Lewis accompanied by his manager Jerry Walls pushed through the crowd to the ring a minute later.

Despite agreeing to allow the stranglehold in all falls originally, Sandow called for banning the stranglehold in the first fall. Lewis and Walls agreed to a coin toss, which Jenkins won. The men agreed not to use the stranglehold during the first fall.[xcix]

Referee Tommy Devereaux called the men to the center of the ring for final instructions at 8:56 p.m. Devereaux started the match at 8:57 p.m.

Fans watched a fast match. Jenkins secured a toehold to start the first fall. Lewis gave up to the hold in only three minutes.

During the first fall, Sandow left the corner coaching Jenkins to "grab his toe." The Lexington Police chased Sandow back to his corner and told him that leaving his authorized area during the rest of the match would cause the police to remove Sandow from ringside.[c]

During the twenty-minute intermission, Jenkins appeared relaxed while Lewis showed stress and tension. Devereaux called the men back to the stage for the second fall.

Since Lewis could now use the stranglehold, Lewis at once jumped for it. Jenkins broke it and tried for his own stranglehold. For the next nine minutes, Lewis and Jenkins traded stranglehold attempts.

Lewis switched to an armlock and head scissors. Jenkins barely avoided Lewis' pin attempt. The men rolled off the mat and stage down to the floor.

When they stepped back onto the stage, Jenkins tried a crotch hold that Lewis shook off. Lewis pressed his own offense and secured a double-arm wristlock. Jenkins looked done but escaped at the edge of the mat.

As Jenkins stood back up, Lewis was finally able to wrap his arm around

Jenkins neck. Lewis squeezed as Jenkins' face turned ashen. Jenkins tapped his surrender to the stranglehold at fourteen minutes.[ci]

The scene in the dressing rooms switched for both men. Lewis now appeared loose, while Jenkins stalked nervously around the room.

Since Jenkins scored the quickest fall, Lewis could not use the stranglehold during the third fall. However, Lewis did not appear concerned.

Jenkins stepped on stage with a visibly swollen throat and neck. Lewis applied a neck-yoke to start the third fall but Jenkins surprised Lewis and the crowd by breaking the hold.

Jenkins' small victory was short-lived as the stranglehold had visibly weakened Jenkins for the second fall. Jenkins avoided a second neck-yoke to the cheers of the Lexington crowd, who were turning on local wrestler Lewis.

"Billy" Jenkins, of Wichita, Kans.,

Figure 18- Billy Jenkins circa 1913. Billy Sandow brought Jenkins to Kentucky to challenge Ed "Strangler" Lewis (Public Domain)

    Lewis secured a third neck-yoke, and this time Jenkins could not escape. Lewis pinned Jenkins at five minutes of the third fall to take the two-out-of-three-falls match.[cii]

After the match, Walls announced that Lewis would wrestle Gus Kuvaris in Louisville on December 19, 1913. Lewis would also wrestle Charles Challender, "The Mysterious Conductor," on Christmas Day 1913.

Lewis crushed Kuvaris in straight falls at Louisville's Buckingham Theater. Lewis used the stranglehold to force Kuvaris to give up both the first and second falls in thirty-two minutes and fourteen minutes, respectively.[ciii]

On Christmas Night 1913, Lewis and Jenkins drew the largest crowd in Lexington to that point. The Lexington Opera House held about 1,000 spectators. We can use this number as the approximate attendance.

The reporter for the Lexington Herald said that organizers placed 225 chairs on the stage, or spectators would have filled all the theater seats. One hundred ladies made up part of the crowd.^civ

The match drew the crowd despite an on-going snowstorm. The match could have drawn 1,225 spectators without the winter weather.

Jenkins entered the stage area first with his manager Billy Sandow. Lewis again entered second with Jerry Walls. For this match, Wallace Yeager served as referee.

Yeager started the match at 9:15 p.m. Lewis led at first and applied a head chancery, but Jenkins slipped the hold. Both men fell to the mat but scrambled back to their feet.

Jenkins dove for a toe hold which Lewis countered with a body scissors. Jenkins squirmed out of his predicament. As Jenkins tried to escape, Lewis grabbed his own toe hold.

Jenkins countered by applying his own toe hold. The wrestlers looked like they were playing footsie for a minute before Lewis broke loose and stood back to his feet.

Jenkins dove for another toe hold but Lewis kicked loose. Jenkins looked worn out and did not put up much of a challenge for the rest of the match.

In the ensuing ten minutes, Lewis drug Jenkins off the stage, when Jenkins tried for another toe hold. Lewis also tackled Jenkins off the stage when Lewis tried for a double-leg takedown.

Sandow yelled for Jenkins to secure another toe hold but Jenkins looked helpless from exhaustion. Sandow grabbed his own hair in frustration.

Lewis put on a double-arm wristlock and forced Jenkins to his knees. Jenkins looked over at Yaeger and tapped out to the wristlock in thirty minutes.[cv]

Jenkins wrestled desperately to start the second fall. Jenkins applied a head scissors on Lewis, who slipped the hold with ease.

Jenkins tried vainly to apply the toe hold but Lewis had no problem escaping the attempts. Lewis applied another double wristlock to set up his neck-yoke. Lewis used the neck-yoke to cause Jenkins to give up for the second fall and match at twenty-two minutes of the second fall.[cvi]

Lewis' performance impressed one important person, Billy Sandow. Sandow said, "Lewis is the fastest wrestler the world has ever seen. He is unquestionably the greatest mat man in the United States. I am prepared to give him $5,000 for one year's service if he will accept my offer. I thought Jenkins would beat him, but now I know Lewis is his master. He is faster than Frank Gotch ever was. He's a wonder."[cvii]

The Lexington fans and reporters were dismissive of Sandow's overture, but they should have taken it more seriously. Sandow saw something special in Lewis and did not intend to stop with one offer to be Lewis' manager.

For now, Walls was still Lewis' manager and arranged for a Chicago match with Gus "Americus" Schoenlein in Chicago, Illinois on Monday, December 29, 1913.

"Americus" helped Dr. Roller train Georg Hackenschmidt for his second match with Frank Gotch in 1911. A skilled national level wrestler in his own right, "Americus" competed for both the World Title and the American Title in the past.

Gotch was furious with Schoenlein for working with Hackenschmidt in 1911. In 1912, Gotch wrestled one of his few contests after winning the Hackenschmidt rematch when he defended the World Heavyweight Wrestling Championship against "Americus." Gotch legitimately injured Schoenlein's ankle with a toe hold as a receipt for helping Hackenschmidt.[cviii]

Schoenlein had a bigger reputation than Lewis at this point in their careers. "Americus" won the match in two straight falls. Despite the loss, Lewis entered 1914 with the promise of another good year.

Figure 19- Billy Jenkins circa 1913 (Public Domain)

Chapter 8 – Still in Kentucky to Start 1914

Lewis was back in Kentucky to start 1914. Lewis remained based in Kentucky but started spending more time wrestling in other states particularly as the year went on.

Jerry M. Walls still managed Lewis in addition to promoting Lexington and Louisville, Kentucky. Walls did not know it but his days as Lewis' manager were numbered.

After the Chicago match with Americus, Lewis returned to Wisconsin for the first time in at least a year. For the first time, the Lexington newspapers acknowledged that Lewis hailed from Wisconsin and not Lexington.[cix] As Lewis traveled north, Walls traveled south back to Lexington to set up a couple of matches with Dr. Benjamin Roller.

Dr. Roller agreed to wrestle Billy Jenkins in a spot show at Paris, Kentucky on Monday, January 5, 1914. Walls booked Dr. Roller to wrestle William Demetral at the Lexington Opera House on Tuesday, January 6, 1914. Lewis agreed to return to Lexington by January 6th to referee the Demetral-Roller match. Lewis refereed the match without incident.

Lewis took a few bookings outside of Kentucky. On January 8th, Lewis traveled to Cincinnati to wrestle former opponent, Gus Kuvaris. Lewis used the stranglehold to take the first fall in fifty minutes. The stranglehold sapped Kuvaris so badly that he surrendered the match to Lewis instead of returning for the second fall.[cx]

On January 9, 1914, Lewis wrestled Jack Stone at the Buckingham Theater in Louisville, Kentucky. Of all Lewis' Kentucky opponents, Walls and Barton promotion of Jack Stone is hard to understand.

After Lewis beat Dr. Roller and Demetral, Lewis should have crushed Stone in straight falls. Yet, Walls and Barton continued booking Stone strong.

Strong won the first fall in thirty-six minutes with a body scissors and double-arm wristlock. Prior to scoring the fall, Stone punished Lewis with a toe hold.[cxi]

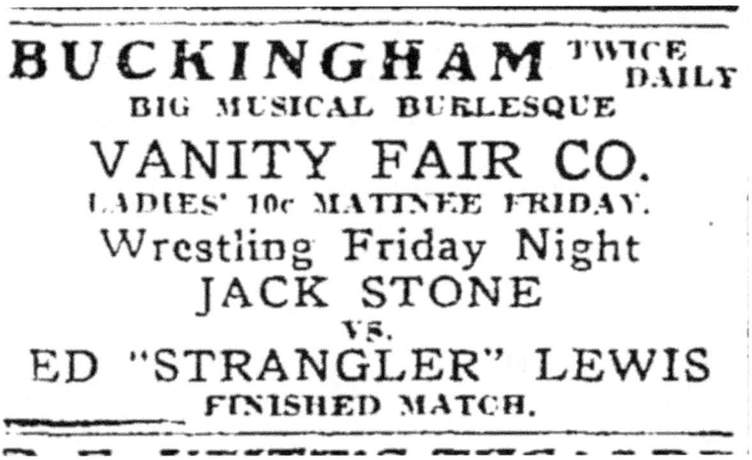

BUCKINGHAM TWICE DAILY
BIG MUSICAL BURLESQUE
VANITY FAIR CO.
LADIES' 10c MATINEE FRIDAY.
Wrestling Friday Night
JACK STONE
vs.
ED "STRANGLER" LEWIS
FINISHED MATCH.

Figure 20- Newspaper advertisement for Jack Stone vs. "Strangler" Lewis (Public Domain)

Lewis dominated Stone in the second fall. Lewis used a head scissors to pin Stone at thirty minutes, thirty seconds of the second fall.

Lewis and Stone wrestled for an hour and four minutes during the third fall without a result. The men agreed to a draw. Outside of his first far from dominant defeat of Stone, Lewis either lost or drew with Stone in every later match.

The newspaper report for the *Lexington Herald* said Lewis' decision to wrestle Kuvaris in Cincinnati the night before may have led to Lewis' listless performance during the first fall.^{cxii}

Three days later, Lewis wrestled Charles Challender, "the Mysterious Conductor," at the Lexington Opera House. The January 12th match was the first time Challender, a popular Chicago wrestler, visited Kentucky.

Challender utilized a ju-jitsu armlock as his finishing move. Lewis as usual would be hunting for the stranglehold.

The men entered the stage area at 9:00 p.m. Dr. Benjamin Roller refereed this match. Interestingly, Roller called all bets off before starting the match at 9:07 p.m.^{cxiii}

Lewis spent the early part of the match trying to apply his stranglehold, but Challender avoided the move early on.

Challender tried for his own stranglehold, but Lewis easily avoided it. Challender did secure the neck-yoke, but Lewis broke it as well.

Lewis finally applied the stranglehold, but Challender broke it by picking Lewis up and slamming Lewis to the mat. It was Challender's last bit of offense.

Lewis kept squeezing Challender's neck every chance he got. At one point, both men fell over the footlights.

When they stepped back onto the stage, Lewis grabbed a stranglehold. Challender did not have any fight left and signaled his surrender to Dr. Roller. Lewis won the first fall in fifty-six minutes.[cxiv]

Challender complained about the stranglehold during the break. The hold sucked all the energy out of Challender. At least that is what Lewis and Challender wanted us to believe.

When Dr. Roller started the match for the second fall, Lewis only needed seven minutes to force Challender to give up to the stranglehold. Lewis won the match in two straight falls.[cxv]

One of the unique aspects of this match was the Lexington crowd cheering for Challender instead of the Lexington based Lewis. Lewis' use of the controversial stranglehold was turning the fans against Lewis.

Lewis was back on the road to wrestle a rematch against Gus Kuvaris at Cincinnati's Standard Theater on Thursday, January 15, 1914. Lewis agreed not to use the stranglehold. Lewis pinned Kuvaris in twenty-nine minutes for the first fall.

During the second fall, Lewis threw Kuvaris headfirst to the mat. Kuvaris told the referee he could not continue as the slam knocked Kuvaris dizzy. The referee awarded the match to Lewis due to Kuvaris' withdrawal.[cxvi]

On Friday, January 23, 1914, Lewis returned to Kentucky and wrestled Dr. Benjamin F. Roller in the hyped rematch.

The match proved to be a controversial one.

Lewis and Roller entered the stage area of the Lexington Opera House. After a prolonged discussion, the wrestlers selected Wallace Yaeger, a frequent Lexington referee, to officiate the match.

Lewis and Roller agreed not to use their pet holds, the stranglehold and toe hold, respectively. Lewis proved to be the aggressor, while Roller looked for his opportunities to counter Lewis' offense.

Twice within the first ten minutes, Lewis and Roller rolled off the mat, past the footlights, and out into the seats on either side of the stage. The second time, the older, out-of-shape editor of one of the local newspapers gave the wrestlers a thorough tongue lashing for almost landing on him.[cxvii]

Dr. Roller took Lewis down to the mat, but Lewis bridged Roller up and off him to the cheers of the fans. Lewis' athletic exhibition impressed even the jaded newspaper reporters at mat side.

Lewis applied a neck-yoke, which Dr. Roller broke by jumping off the stage into the seats. The newspaper reporters and fans dodged flying wrestlers all evening.

Roller took the rare offensive after forty minutes of wrestling. Roller dove for a crotch hold, picked Lewis up off the mat, and dumped Lewis back down to the mat. Both of Lewis' shoulders struck the mat for the first fall at forty-one minutes.[cxviii]

To start the second fall, Lewis applied his neck-yoke. Roller complained that Lewis was strangling him. Yaeger said the hold was legal.

After Roller broke the neck-yoke, Roller used the stranglehold on Lewis. Lewis responded by strangling Roller back. Yaeger again did not take any action as the Lexington Police approached the ring.

When Lewis and Roller ended up by the footlights, Yaeger feared the men would roll into the crowd again. Yaeger tried to stop them, but Roller tried to throw Yaeger over the footlights.

The Lexington Police looked ready to stop the match when Lewis secured his neck-yoke. Roller struggled valiantly but signaled his surrender to Yaeger at twenty-one minutes of the second fall.[cxix] Lewis tied the match at one fall apiece.

Lewis and Roller traded neck-yokes to start the third fall. Neither man could gain an advantage. After seven minutes, Roller picked Lewis up and slammed Lewis to the mat. Yaeger signaled that Roller had pinned Lewis although everyone in the building, but the official agreed Lewis' shoulders were not down on the mat.[cxx]

The *Lexington Herald* called Roller's win a "fluke victory."[cxxi] Fans were demanding a rematch between Lewis and Roller, which was music to Jerry Walls' ears.

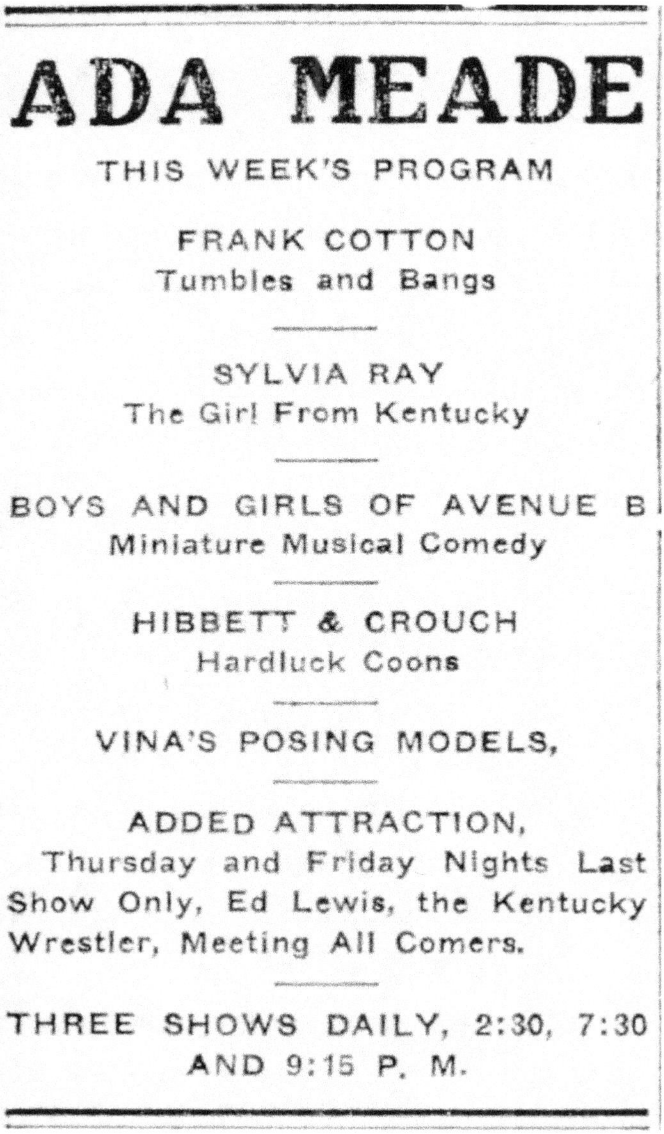

ADA MEADE

THIS WEEK'S PROGRAM

FRANK COTTON
Tumbles and Bangs

SYLVIA RAY
The Girl From Kentucky

BOYS AND GIRLS OF AVENUE B
Miniature Musical Comedy

HIBBETT & CROUCH
Hardluck Coons

VINA'S POSING MODELS,

ADDED ATTRACTION,
Thursday and Friday Nights Last Show Only, Ed Lewis, the Kentucky Wrestler, Meeting All Comers.

THREE SHOWS DAILY, 2:30, 7:30 AND 9:15 P. M.

Figure 21-Ad for Ed "Strangler" Lewis taking on all-comers at the Ada Meade Theater (Public Domain)

On Friday, January 30, 1914, Ed "Strangler" Lewis took part in a rare exhibition by agreeing to wrestle all-comers at the end of the regular vaudeville program at the Ada Meade theater. Promoters occasionally issued these challenges but normally wrestlers only challenge crowd members to wrestle them at the carnival athletic shows.

Unlike the carnival shows, which would move on to the next town, a professional like Lewis had a lot to lose in these challenge matches. If a hot shot amateur like a Joe Stecher showed up, the amateur can embarrass the professional.

Joe Stecher almost pinned Dr. Roller before he graduated high school. Stecher also taught Yussuf Hussane not to mess with the young wunderkind.

Walls and Lewis were taking a risk but it was less of a risk with a skilled "hooker" like Lewis. If an amateur showed up, Lewis could "hook", apply a submission hold, on the challenger.

Lexington Police Officer Lawrence Piercy stepped up to challenge Lewis. Piercy weighed one hundred seventy-five pounds to Lewis' two hundred pounds.

Piercy lasted six minutes before Lewis pinned Piercy. Lewis could have just been exercising caution in the challenge. However, it would be smart of Lewis to carry the officer for five minutes or so before beating Piercy to keep good relations with the Lexington Police.[cxxii]

Lewis was back in the ring with a professional on Tuesday, February 3, 1914. Lewis wrestled a rematch with Charles Challender, "the Mysterious Conductor," at the Lexington Opera House. Newspaper reporters covering the match called it the "most scientific match" ever seen in Lexington.[cxxiii]

Bob Rogers, the sporting editor of the *Louisville Herald*, refereed the match. Rogers started the match at 9:03 p.m.

To start the match, Lewis took Challender to the mat with a head chancery. Challender scrambled back to his feet causing both men to roll off the stage. Rogers directed the men to come back onto the stage and tie up in the center of the ring.[cxxiv]

Challender tried to apply the jujitsu armlock on Lewis, but Lewis ripped his arm out of each attempt. Lewis in turn tried to put the neck-yoke on Challender.

Challender switched to the toehold after about twenty minutes of wrestling. Challender nearly secured the hold two or three times, but Lewis kicked out each attempt.

Lewis went for a toehold of his own twice before applying a head scissors and armlock on Challender. It looked dire for Challender for about five minutes. Challender eventually escaped the near fall.

Lewis then applied a double-arm wristlock. Rogers asked Challender two or three times if he wanted to give up. Challender shook his head "No." Challender pulled his arm out right before Lewis could force the arm back at an unnatural angle.

Challender rolled to Lewis' legs and took Lewis to the mat with a leg grapevine. Challender applied the toehold, which Lewis could not break. Lewis verbally gave up to the holds as Rogers signaled the end to the first fall at forty-five minutes.[cxxv]

Before the second fall, Rogers told the crowd that the match was the most scientific he ever officiated. The fans cheered Rogers' statement and gave both Lewis and Challender a standing ovation to start the second fall.

Lewis pressed the action from the start of the second fall. Lewis applied his first neck-yoke seventeen minutes into the second fall. Challender wilted from the pressure of the hold.

Figure 22- Fred Beell circa December 1906 when Beell "defeated" Frank Gotch for the American Heavyweight Wrestling Championship (Public Domain)

Lewis continued pressing Challender throughout the second fall and pinned Challender with a neck-yoke in thirty-four minutes. Challender's seconds helped Challender back to the dressing room for the twenty-minute intermission.

Challender could not recover during the intermission. Lewis needed one minute in the third fall to pin Challender with a double waist lock.[cxxvi] The fans cheered Challender, who put up a much better effort in the rematch with Lewis.

Lewis continued to tour outside of Kentucky as Walls arranged for Lewis to wrestle Fred Beell, a nationally known wrestler, in Chicago, Illinois. Beell held a victory over Frank Gotch in December 1906.

Gotch worked the match with Beell, who beat Gotch for the American Heavyweight Wrestling Championship, when Gotch struck his head on a ring post. Gotch was so convincing that only a few newspaper reporters pointed out what a preposterous accident led to Gotch's defeat. Unsurprisingly, Gotch won the title back from Beell seventeen days later.

As Lewis prepared to leave for Chicago, Lewis was still wrestling challenge matches at Lexington's Ada Meade Theater after the last vaudeville performance. On Thursday, February 5, 1914, two days after the match with Challender, Billy Sandow surprised Lewis and Walls by challenging Lewis to a match.[cxxvii]

Sandow had been a professional wrestler but campaigned as a lightweight wrestler. Lewis had a significant weight advantage of thirty pounds over Sandow.

Lewis offered any local wrestler one dollar per minute if they could keep Lewis from pinning them. If the challenger lasted fifteen minutes, Lewis agreed to give the challenger twenty-five dollars.

Sandow displayed toughness and determination by spending ten minutes with Lewis. Sandow also continued trying to lure Lewis away from Walls.[cxxviii]

Lewis still refused to leave Walls, so Sandow brought in a wrestler to test

Lewis. Lewis agreed to wrestle "the unknown" on Tuesday, February 10, 1914.

Walls made a puzzling decision about the challenge of "the unknown." Walls banned the stranglehold for the match.

Sandow remarked that it was odd to ban Lewis' pet hold. Sandow told the local newspapers that Walls suspected who Sandow's challenger was going to be. Since the wrestler knew the stranglehold as well as Lewis, Walls banned the hold for the challenge match.[cxxix]

On Monday, February 9, 1914, Lewis returned to Chicago to wrestle Fred Beell. The men met at the Empire Theater, the usual site for Empire Club wrestling cards.

Lewis won the first fall in nine minutes, thirty-seven seconds with a wrist lock and crotch hold. Beell won the second fall with a headlock at eleven minutes, thirty-one seconds. Beell took the third fall and match with a reverse toe hold and cross-body lock at ten minutes, thirty-five seconds.[cxxx]

Lewis' losing streak in Illinois continued. Lewis returned to Kentucky on Tuesday, February 10th, to wrestle Billy Sandow's "the Unknown" at the Lexington Opera House. The unknown turned out to be Marin Plestina.[cxxxi]

Martin "Farmer" Burns trained Plestina for a professional wrestling career. Plestina debuted in 1910 and was three years older than Lewis. Plestina was a hooker, who was dangerous in a legitimate contest.

Despite being two of the best hookers in professional wrestling, Lewis and Plestina worked the challenge match at Lexington. Wallace Yaeger refereed the match.

Before the men tied up, Billy Sandow and Jerry Walls argued over the stranglehold. Sandow wanted to allow it. Walls insisted on banning the hold. Eventually, Sandow gave up and the match started with Yaeger telling the wrestlers that they could not use the stranglehold.[cxxxii]

A fan could be forgiven for believing Lewis and Plestina wrestled a contest because the match developed into a boring stalemate. Lewis and Plestina traded toeholds and neck-yokes during the match. After two hours, Yaeger declared the match a draw. The fans cheered the efforts of both men despite the inconclusive outcome.[cxxxiii]

Fan interest in a rematch led Jerry Walls to book a return match for Wednesday, February 18, 1914, at the Lexington Opera House. Walls selected Heywood Allen of Louisville to referee the match. Allen would later promote professional wrestling in Louisville, Kentucky.

Allen figured in the match early, when Plestina started using rough house tactics. Lewis responded by driving Plestina off the mat, past the edge of the state, and into the chairs.

Upon returning to the mat, the wrestlers again started rough housing.

Lewis drove Plestina off the stage. The momentum took Lewis off the stage also.

Allen called both men to the center of the mat. Allen warned both wrestlers that any more fouls would cause Allen to disqualify the offending wrestler.[cxxxiv]

Lewis and Plestina wrestled cleanly for ten more minutes before Lewis applied a headlock. Lewis refused to release the hold at the edge of the mat.

Allen warned Lewis repeatedly to release the hold. After Lewis ignored Allen three to four times, Allen disqualified Lewis for the first fall.[cxxxv]

After a twenty-minute intermission, Allen started the second fall. Lewis and Plestina tied up for about five minutes before Plestina picked up Lewis, and slammed Lewis to the mat for the second fall and match.

Lewis struck his head on the mat, which no one realized at first. After Allen awarded the fall to Plestina, Allen, Plestina, and the managers realized Lewis was not moving. A doctor came onto the stage to aid Lewis.^{cxxxvi}

Newspaper reports carried Lewis' exploits nationwide. The coverage helped build Lewis' reputation as a future contender, but he still lost almost half his matches. A new manager made a big difference.

Figure 23- Marin Plestina (Public Domain)

Chapter 9 — Branching Out into Alabama

On Friday, February 27, 1914, Ed "Strangler" Lewis wrestled his first match in Birmingham, Alabama. Promoters booked Lewis and another wrestler to take on Dr. Benjamin F. Roller in a handicapped match. Roller would have to defeat both wrestlers or lose the match.

Roller defeated the local wrestler. Roller was not able to pin Lewis costing him the match.[cxxxvii] Lewis won the match to setup a potential rematch.

The Birmingham promoters started to build Lewis up by leaking a story to Birmingham newspaper reporters about Lewis wrestling a bear in Chicago.[cxxxviii] If Lewis wrestled a bear in Chicago, the Chicago newspapers missed it. Wrestling promoters and managers used fanciful tales, which reporters could not prove or disprove, to build up their wrestlers from the earliest days of the sport.

Charges of "faking" or working the matches dogged the sport as well. In

October 1913, Chicago authorities arrested William Demetral for taking part in a fake wrestling match in Toledo, Ohio, on September 1, 1913. A photographer brought the charges as he felt Demetral and "the wrestling syndicate based out of Chicago" bilked the photographer out of the bets placed on the match.[cxxxix]

The photographer William A. Schmidt claimed the bets totaled four thousand dollars. Demetral told Schmidt that he was going to purposely lose a match in Toledo. Schmidt traveled with Demetral to Toledo.

Schmidt placed the bet on Demetral's opponent. Demetral lost the first fall but after thirty minutes of wrestling Demetral's opponent passed out. The referee awarded Demetral the match costing Schmidt four thousand dollars.

Rightly suspecting that he had been bilked, Schmidt went to Chicago authorities and reported the fraud.

Chicago prosecutors arrested Demetral and charged him with fraud.

Later, Schmidt dropped the case, as the victim was also a perpetrator. Scmidt intended to collude with Demetral and the promoters to bilk other gamblers.

Birmingham promoters refused to book Demetral though because of the Chicago charges. The promoters did not want to invite rumors of their putting on fake matches.

On Friday, March 6, 1914, Lewis was supposed to wrestle Martensen Klemm. However, Klemm notified the Birmingham Athletic Club, promoters of the card, that a big wrestler fell on him during a Macon, Georgia match. Klemm could not make the match with Lewis.

The Birmingham Athletic Club contacted Jerry Walls, who agreed that Lewis could wrestle Bob Allen and Gus Kuvaris in a four-out-of-six-falls handicap match. Lewis agreed to throw both Allen and Kuvaris twice in six falls or Allen and Kuvaris would win the match.^{cxl}

Lewis wrestled Kuvaris first. Kuvaris wrestled defensively but it did him little good. Lewis won the first fall with a toehold. After a short intermission, Lewis used another toehold to take the second fall.

Allen stayed away from toeholds, so Lewis used a head scissors and arm hold trap for the third fall. Unlike Kuvaris, Allen took the offensive and had Lewis in trouble a couple of times. Lewis secured another head scissors and arm hold trap to take the fourth and final fall.^{cxli}

Based off Lewis' strong showing, the Birmingham promoters wanted to secure a match with Stanislaus Zbyskzo, who would soon return to Poland.

Figure 24- Artist Rendering of Ed "Strangler" Lewis (Public Domain)

Instead of Zbyszko, the promoters secured a match with Dr. Benjamin Roller for Monday, March 16, 1914, at the Jefferson Theater. Roller and Lewis wrestled evenly for the first hour and twelve minutes.

Roller secured a toehold forcing Lewis to the mat for a pinfall. The hold injured Lewis, who visibly limped back to the dressing room.

A doctor wanted to examine Lewis, but Lewis waved him away. Lewis declared that he would finish the match no matter what.[cxlii]

Lewis tried but Roller quickly secured another toehold. Roller forced Lewis to give up winning the match in two straight falls.[cxliii] It was Roller's most dominant win over Lewis in some time.

After Roller forced Lewis to give up, Jerry Walls jumped up onto the mat. Billy Sandow, who was managing Roller, also jumped onto the mat. Sandow shoved Walls to the floor causing the Birmingham Police to invade the mat area.

After separating the managers, both Walls and Sandow told the officers they were caught up in the match and did not mean to harm the other. The officers released Walls and Sandow with a warning.^{cxliv}

Lewis travelled back to Kentucky for a couple of matches after the Roller match. Lewis wrestled his first match against Chief Two Feathers at the Buckingham Theater on Friday, March 20, 1914.

Lewis won the first fall using his stranglehold in twenty-two minutes. Lewis forced Chief Two Feathers to give up a second time to the stranglehold in thirty-two minutes.^{cxlv} Lewis wrestled one of the most significant matches o his young career three days later.

On Monday, March 23, 1914, Lewis wrestled Stanislaus Zbyszko at Ben Ali Theater in Lexington, Kentucky. Prior to researching this book, I believed that Lewis wrestled Zbyszko for the first time in 1921. However, Lewis wrestled Zbyszko in one of his last matches during

Zbyszko's first tour of the United States from 1909-1914.

In the 1920s, when Lewis dominated professional wrestling and all insiders considered him the greatest wrestler and hooker, Lewis felt only two wrestlers could defeat him in a legitimate contest. Lewis named his training partner Joseph "Toots" Mondt and Stanislaus Zbyszko as the only wrestlers who could defeat Lewis in a "shoot" or legitimate contest.

Zbyszko was eleven years older than Lewis. Zbyszko was also in his early forties at the time. Imagine how good Stanislaus Zbyszko was in 1914 at only thirty-four years of age.

In 1914, Lewis was not on Zbyszko's level. Zbyszko agreed to throw Lewis twice in an hour or lose his part of the gate receipts to Lewis. Zbyszko came to regret his decision.

Zbyszko pursued Lewis throughout the first fall trying to secure a toehold. Lewis continually kicked free and at one time flipped Zbyszko over Lewis' head.

Lewis tried little offense of his own as he realized his skills were not on Zbyszko's level. Zbyszko wrestled according to Greco-Roman wrestling rules prior to wrestling in the United States. Zbyszko learned catch-as-catch-can wrestling after arriving here to challenge Frank Gotch.

If Zbyszko had more catch wrestling experience, he could have pinned Lewis much quicker. Instead, it took Zbyszko forty-three minutes to force Lewis to give up to the toehold.[cxlvi] Zbyszko still felt confident he could pin Lewis a second time in the next seventeen minutes.

Heywood Allen, future Louisville promoter, served as referee for the match. Throughout the match, Allen called the time in five-minute increments. Allen's judgment caused controversy after the match.

When the men stepped back onto the mat, Lewis knew that he could not pin Zbyszko. Instead of engaging with Zbyszko, Lewis wrestled defensively.

Over the next fifteen minutes, if Zbyszko threatened to apply a hold, Lewis simply ran off the mat. Zbyszko complained about Lewis running away, but Allen told him the rules allowed Lewis' tactics.[cxlvii]

Allen would call Lewis back to the mat and Lewis would come back to the mat without delay. Evading Zbyszko's offense, Lewis lasted the sixty minutes and took Zbyszko's part of the gate receipts.

Zbyszko was furious and complained about Lewis continuously running off the mat. Allen told Zbyszko that he should have requested the ring be roped off, which Zbyszko could do under the rules. If Lewis returned to the mat, Allen could not disqualify Lewis.[cxlviii]

The million-dollar question is whether Zbyszko and Lewis worked the match or wrestled a legitimate contest. Zbyszko may have only worked one match to build up his championship match with Frank Gotch in 1910 during his first tour of America.

Based on Zbyszko's reaction and Lewis running off the mat to escape Zbyszko beating him, the men wrestled a legitimate contest. The men would not meet for eight more years. They would work those matches.

On Friday, March 27, 1914, Walls booked Lewis to wrestle William Demetral. However, Demetral claimed Zbyszko injured him earlier in the week. Emile Bruggelo substituted for Demetral. Lewis defeated Bruggelo in two straight falls after carrying Bruggelo for almost thirty minutes.

On Monday, March 30, 1914, Lewis wrestled the giant Russian wrestler, Ivan Mamutoff at the Ben Ali Theater in Lexington, Kentucky. Mamutoff weighed over three hundred pounds.

Mamutoff threw Lewis around the mat, but it seemed to amuse Lewis. Lewis grabbed Mamutoff with an arm roll and turned Mamutoff onto his back for the first fall in nineteen minutes.[cxlix]

Lewis needed less than three minutes to use a second arm roll to turn Mamutoff to the mat for the second fall and match in straight falls. March ended well for Lewis. To start his April campaign Lewis traveled to another southern state as he continued to take bookings outside of Kentucky.

Figure 25- Stanislaus Zbyszko in 1914 (Public Domain)

Chapter 10 – First Match in Georgia

On Wednesday, April 1, 1914, Ed "Strangler" Lewis wrestled his first match in Georgia. Lewis wrestled Jack Leon for the "Championship of the South" at the Opera House in Macon, Georgia.[cl]

Leon won the first fall with a half-Nelson and crotch hold in forty-five minutes, twenty seconds. Fans applauded both men's efforts.

Lewis evened up the match up with his neck yoke at thirty-two minutes, twelve seconds. Leon showed visible concern at the end of the second fall.

Leon told his manager W. H. Barton, the former Lexington promoter, that he did not think he could beat Lewis. Barton told him the neck-yoke was just a three quarters Nelson. Barton said, "Just keep your elbows close to him all the time, Jack."[cli]

Leon followed the advice and kept Lewis from applying his new hold. Leon won the third fall with a crotch hold in twenty-three minutes, fifteen seconds. Lewis shook Leon's hand after Leon beat him. The fans cheered both wrestlers as they left the mat side.

Lewis kept up his busy touring schedule by wrestling Billy Edwards in Cincinnati, Ohio on Thursday, April 2, 1914. Lewis defeated Edwards in two straight falls.[clii]

On Friday, April 3, 1914, Lewis was back in Louisville, Kentucky to wrestle the "Champion of the Pacific Northwest" Tom Dodge. Dodge did not quite live up to his billing as Lewis defeated Dodge easily.

Lewis won the first fall in fourteen minutes with a body scissors and toe hold combination. Lewis won the second fall and match in three minutes with a hammerlock.[cliii]

In the meantime, Jerry Walls booked another match between Ed "Strangler" Lewis and William Demetral for Louisville, Kentucky on Friday, April 10, 1914. To secure his booking, Demetral posted $100 with the sporting editor of *the Courier-Journal*.^{cliv} Walls was still smarting from Demetral's earlier cancellations and demanded an appearance bond going forward.

While Walls negotiated with Demetral, Lewis was in Detroit, Michigan on April 7, 1914, to wrestle Zbyszko but it was not Stanislaus. Lewis wrestled Wladek Zbyszko for the first time.

While Lewis always respected Stanislaus Zbyszko, Lewis detested Wladek Zbyszko. When an opponent angered Lewis, it usually resulted in Lewis punching the offending party. Lewis did not cripple his opponents with one of his hooks like Evan "Strangler" Lewis did although Ed "Strangler" Lewis easily could.

Legend has it that Lewis made one exception, when Lewis injured Wladek Zbyszko's shoulder with a double-arm wristlock in Rochester, New York around 1917. It is still a legend in my mind because I have not yet found the evidence for this match.

However, plenty of evidence exists for their matches devolving into fist fights. The animosity between the men may have in their first match in Detroit. Lewis wrestled Zbyszko in front of a little under a thousand fans at the Armory.

Lewis and Wladek Zbyszko spent the first twenty minutes pulling and tugging at each other. Lewis yelled to the referee that Zbyszko tried to gouge Lewis' eye. After stepping back six to eight inches, Lewis hit Zbyszko in the jaw with a right cross.[clv]

The blow dropped Zbyszko to his knees as the Detroit Police rushed the ring. Zbyszko tried to charge Lewis, but Lewis dropped Zbyszko to the mat with another punch.

Lewis' and Zbyszko's seconds also started fighting. The Detroit Police separated all the parties as the crowd started to riot. Detroit was home to a large Polish population, who did not like Lewis punching the daylights out of Wladek Zbyszko.

Zbyszko addressed the crowd in Polish denying that he gouged Lewis' eyes. Fans tried to attack Lewis as Lewis left the stage, but the Detroit Police escorted Lewis safely to the dressing room. It took the Detroit Police an hour to clear the arena.[clvi] The police arrested a dozen spectators for brawling in the crowd.

Lewis' and Zbyszko's brawl made the front page of newspapers across the United States. The reaction figured into Lewis' rematch with William Demetral although Lewis and Demetral worked their fight.

When Lewis and Demetral each won one fall apiece in their Friday, April 10th match at Louisville's Buckingham Theater, Lewis and Demetral started the third fall by punching each other. After a Louisville Police Detective stopped the match, Lewis and Demetral continued their fight with Lewis blooding Demetral's nose.clvii Demetral did not mind because he believed the rematch with Lewis would lead to a huge payday.

Walls planned to use the fisticuffs to build the rematch. Early results were good as a large crowd waited for Lewis outside the theater. When Lewis appeared, the fans gave him a loud ovation.

Before wrestling Demetral again, Lewis traveled to Buffalo, New York to wrestle a rematch with Wladek Zbyszko on Thursday, April 23, 1914. The men wrestled at the Broadway Auditorium.

In this match, Lewis and Zbyszko controlled their tempers. After an hour, Zbyszko picked up Lewis with a crotch hold and slammed Lewis to the mat. Lewis struck his head on the mat and could not continue. The referee awarded the match to Zbyszko at one hour, seven minutes, and twenty seconds.clviii

Despite the animosity between them, Lewis and Zbyszko could work together to put on a good match occasionally. Zbyszko did not anger Lewis this time, so Lewis did not punch Zbyszko in the face. Too bad Zbyszko could not maintain his good behavior.

Figure 26-Ed "Strangler" Lewis in Spring 1914 (Public Domain)

On Monday, April 27, 1914, Lewis wrestled Charlie Cutler at the Ben Ali Theater in Lexington, Kentucky. A large crowd attended the marque match up with the nationally known Cutler.

Heywood Allen refereed the match. Allen announced to the crowd that Lewis could not use the stranglehold in this match.[clix] After checking both wrestlers, Allen started the match at 9:10 p.m.

Lewis tried to get behind Cutler, but Cutler kept Lewis in front of him to start the match. After wrestling for about ten minutes, Lewis finally got behind Cutler.

Lewis thought he had the victory with a toe hold. Cutler broke the hold at the last-minute countering with a head chancery.

As the men stood back to their feet, they began roughhousing. Allen warned both wrestlers that he would not hesitate to disqualify them if the rough tactics continued.

Lewis jumped for a headlock, but Cutler countered. Lewis then drove both he and Cutler off the stage into the mat side chairs. Allen warned Lewis that one more foul would cause Allen to disqualify Lewis.

Lewis wrestled cleanly after the hard warning. Lewis finally got Cutler down and used the toe hold to force Cutler to give up for the first fall at the twenty-five-minute mark.[clx]

Cutler walked over to Lewis' dressing room and told Lewis that Lewis had improved one hundred percent since their match in Chicago the previous year. Lewis and Cutler shook hands and prepared for the second fall.

Cutler started the second fall with more urgency and showed more offense. Cutler secured a half-Nelson and crotch hold before switching to a leg scissors and hammerlock. Lewis slipped all the holds.

After about twenty minutes of wrestling, Cutler used a crotch lift to dump Lewis to the mat. Lewis struck his head on the mat and lost consciousness for less than a minute. Allen awarded Cutler the second fall at twenty-four minutes.[clxi]

The third fall proved to be a short affair. Cutler applied a half-Nelson, but Lewis broke the hold. Lewis then applied his neck-yoke.

It looked direr for Cutler, but Cutler finally broke the hold. Lewis burned up all his energy trying to end the match.

Cutler applied a leg bar, arm, and headlock with further arm hold. Lewis struggled mightily but Cutler kept on the pressure. Cutler pinned Lewis in nine minutes, forty seconds for the third fall and match.[clxii] Lewis wrestled valiantly but was not on Cutler's level yet.

The dog days of summer were approaching quickly forcing Walls to book the end of Lewis' current tour in Kentucky. Walls announced that Lewis planned to set up a summer training camp in Lansing, Iowa. Walls said he would focus on booking the beginning of the fall 1914 Kentucky schedule.

Before Lewis headed to Iowa, Walls secured Lewis another match with Jack Leon in Macon, Georgia. Macon promoter W.H. Barton, the former Lexington promotional partner of Walls, agreed to allow Lewis to use both the stranglehold and neck-yoke in the match.[clxiii]

Barton decided to hold the match in Central City Park due to the hot weather conditions in Macon. Barton felt the fans would be more comfortable outdoors than in the Macon Opera House.

Prior to wrestling Leon, Lewis travelled to Springfield, Massachusetts for a match with Mehmed Sendrelly on Monday, May 11, 1914. The newspaper reporters described the Albanian wrestler Sendrelly as a giant.

Despite his size advantage over Lewis, Lewis defeated Sendrelly in two straight falls at the Springfield Auditorium. Lewis needed forty minutes for the first fall but only eleven minutes to take the second fall.[clxiv]

Lewis hopped a train and made it to Macon, Georgia on the evening of May 12, 1914. After resting for a day, Lewis wrestled Jack Leon on the evening of Thursday, May 14, 1914.

SEASON'S GREATEST WRESTLING MATCH
At Central City Park Tonight

JACK LEON The Southern Champion
and
ED. "Strangler" LEWIS

In the match every hold known to wrestling game including Lewis' famous "strangle" will be allowed.

General Admission 50c   Ringside $1.00

LADIES ADMITTED FREE

First class preliminaries with first bout starting at 8:15
SPECIAL CAR SERVICE

Figure 27- Jack Leon vs. Ed "Strangler" Lewis in Macon, Georgia on Thursday, May 14, 1914 (Public Domain)

Three hundred fans showed up to watch the match, which the newspaper reporters considered a good crowd.[clxv] Professional wrestling was still developing as a spectator sport. Crowds of hundreds were the norm in developing promotions, while other areas like New York or Chicago could draw crowds of a thousand fans or more.

    Despite Leon being the local wrestler, the fans cheered Lewis for five minutes as Lewis entered the mat area of the ballpark. The fans split evenly in supporting Lewis and Leon.

    Leon experienced early success in the match as Leon pinned Lewis with a half-Nelson and crotch hold in forty-eight minutes. However, Lewis evened the match up in short order with the stranglehold.

    Leon staggered back to his corner during the intermission. At the start of the third fall, Lewis applied another stranglehold causing Leon to give up in a couple of minutes.[clxvi] Lewis secured his first victory of Jack Leon.

Lewis addressed the crowd after the match. Lewis told the crowd that Leon proved to be his toughest opponent so far. Lewis further said that not a single professional wrestler, not even Stanislaus Zbyszko, could withstand the effects of the stranglehold.[clxvii]

Lewis agreed to another match in Macon for the following week. Ernest Fimby wrestled primarily in Michigan before traveling south for a match with Lewis on Tuesday, May 19, 1914. Fimby proved no threat to Lewis.

Lewis won the first fall in fourteen minutes with a reverse nelson. Lewis won the second fall in thirty seconds with a single leg takedown, arm scissors, and arm bar.[clxviii]

On Friday, May 21, 1914, Lewis wrestled Leon in a rematch at a spot show in Dublin, Georgia. Lewis won the first fall with the stranglehold in sixteen minutes.[clxix]

Leon evened the match up with a half-Nelson and crotch hold in twenty-six minutes. Lewis won the third fall and match with a second stranglehold.[clxx] After defeating Leon for the second time, Lewis returned to Lexington for the final match of the season against Jack Stone.

Walls booked Lewis to wrestle Stone at the Opera House on Friday, May 29, 1914. In a result that continues to defy logic, Stone wrestled Lewis to a draw. The outcome of this match was a disaster.

Lewis won the first fall in twenty-one minutes with a stranglehold. Stone evened the match at one fall apiece with a body hold in the same twenty-one minutes.[clxxi]

The men wrestled sixteen more minutes before the mat, which the wrestlers ripped to shreds during the match, began to disintegrate. With sawdust covering both wrestlers, referee Tommy Devereaux declared the match a draw because of the torn mat.

The fans began to loudly boo and chanted, "Give us our money back!" Walls had the stagehands drop the curtain as the fans threw seat cushions and demanded their money.^clxxii The reaction brought a rough end to what had been a well-received wrestling season.

    The angry fans were just the first of Jerry Walls' problems entering the summer of 1914. Lewis cut his summer training camp short and took on a new manager. Walls was losing the lucrative management of Ed "Strangler" Lewis.

Figure 28- Jack Leon, who claimed the Southern Championship, and wrestled Lewis in Georgia during the spring of 1914 (Public Domain)

Chapter 11 – Under New Management

Ed "Strangler" Lewis was supposed to spend his summer in Lansing, Iowa training for the upcoming wrestling season in Kentucky. However, Lewis cut his camp short in late June 1914 to wrestle matches in Virginia.

Lewis not only cut his training camp short but Ed White, the Chicago promoter, managed Lewis during his Virginia matches. Lewis wrestled his first match in Virginia with Mike Donelly in Richmond, Virginia on July 3, 1914.

Lewis won the match in two straight falls. Lewis won the first fall in forty-five minutes. Lewis only needed seven minutes to win the second fall and match.[clxxiii]

On July 9, 1914, Ed White sent a telegram to Virginia promoters issuing a challenge from Lewis to Gus Kuvaris and Billy Jenkins. Lewis said he would throw both wrestlers in an hour. Lewis offered to wrestle for the gate receipts.[clxxiv]

Figure 29-Ad for the Lewis vs. Jenkins and Kuvaris match (Public Domain)

Fans knew Gus Kuvaris as Gus Kervaras in Virginia, but it is the same wrestler that Lewis wrestled in the past. On Friday, July 17, 1914, Lewis wrestled Jenkins and Kuvaris at the Roanoke Fair Grounds. One thousand two hundred fans turned out to see the match.[clxxv]

Jenkins agreed to allow the stranglehold, but Kuvaris refused. Promoters banned the hold for the match under the circumstances.

With his pet hold banned, Lewis pinned Billy Jenkins in twenty-nine minutes. However, Lewis could not pin Kuvaris in the remaining thirty-one minutes.[clxxvi] Lewis challenged Kuvaris to a rematch. Fans were none the wiser that the match was to setup a singles match between Lewis and Kuvaris.

On Tuesday, July 21, 1914, Lewis wrestled Swedish wrestler Hjalmar Lundin in Richmond, Virginia. Lewis wrestled Lundin at the Broad Street Ball Park.

Lundin arrived in America as a Greco-Roman wrestling specialist. Lundin proved to be an integral part of the 1915 New York International Wrestling Tournament wrestled primarily by Greco-Roman wrestling rules.

Lundin also adapted to the catch-as-catch-can style of the United States. However, Lundin never achieved the same skill level in catch wrestling. Lundin was definitely not in Lewis' class even though Lewis was only twenty-three years old.

Figure 30- Ad for Lewis vs. Lundin from July 1914 in Virginia (Public Domain)

In this match, Lundin secured the first fall in only thirty seconds because Lundin slipped under Lewis, lifted him in the air, and brought Lewis down to the mat.

Lewis struck his head when Lewis tried to turn out of Lundin's slam. Lewis lost consciousness for thirty seconds. The referee awarded Lundin the first fall.[clxxvii]

Lewis fully recovered for the second fall. Lewis remained on the offensive for the entire fall with Lundin trying to stay away from Lewis. Lewis applied a headlock and arm catch to take the second fall in twenty-nine minutes.

Lewis needed another twenty-three minutes to pin Lundin with a body hold.[clxxviii] Lewis did not have much time to rest during the summer of 1914. Promoters booked Lewis for a match the following night in Norfolk, Virginia.

Lewis was supposed to wrestle George Romanough. Romanough wired promoters that he injured himself during training. Promoters substituted Hjalmar Lundin.

Lewis won the only fall in thirty-seven minutes. Lundin told the referee the first fall injured him. Lundin said he would go on if the fans demanded it.

However, the fans allowed Lundin to retire from the match.^{clxxix}

On Monday, July 27, 1914, Lewis wrestled Gus Kuvaris at the Roanoke Fairgrounds in a two-out-of-three-falls match. Lewis and Kuvaris spent the first fall trading toe hold and stranglehold attempts.

At the forty-five-minute mark, Lewis used a half-Nelson to pin Kuvaris for the first fall. Kuvaris evened up the match with a toe hold at seven minutes of the second fall.^{clxxx}

Kuvaris looked like he would win the match with a second toe hold but Lewis slipped out. After hunting the hold most of the match, Lewis finally secured the stranglehold. Lewis forced Kuvaris to give up to the hold at twenty-one minutes, twenty-eight seconds of the third fall.^{clxxxi}

After the match, Lewis accepted the challenge of Yussuf Hussane. Promoters billed him as Yousoff Hussane in Virginia. Hussane was Martin "Farmer"

Burns' choice to assess 20-year-old Joe Stecher in a legitimate contest during 1913.

Instead of teaching the youngster a lesson, Hussane employed desperate measures to escape an embarrassing tap out to Stecher's leg scissors. Stecher hooked Hussane with a leg scissors around the neck. As Stecher squeezed Hussane's carotid artery and started to put Hussane to sleep, Hussane bit Stecher's leg, an obvious foul.

The referee disqualified Hussane, who refused to continue the match. Stecher impressed Burns, who started to work with and train both Stecher brothers.

Lewis wrestled Hussane on Friday, July 31, 1914, at the Broad Street Ball Park in Richmond, Virginia. Fans sat through a two-and-a-half-hour match to see who won between Lewis and Hussane.

Lewis won the first fall in forty-two minutes. Hussane won the second fall with a stranglehold in sixteen minutes.

Lewis won the third fall and match in an hour.[clxxxii]

Hussane disputed the third fall and challenged Lewis to pin him again. Lewis obliged and pinned Hussane in under a minute. Hussane sheepishly left the ringside.

Richmond promoters announced Lewis would wrestle a giant German wrestler named Sampson on the next card. Sampson weighed two hundred forty-five pounds compared to Lewis' two hundred ten pounds.

In newspaper articles leading up to the match, Sampson's management made the absurd claim that Sampson bested Frank Gotch and Dr. Benjamin Roller.[clxxxiii] When pressed on these claims, the publicist admitted that Gotch and Roller won the matches after Sampson gave them all they could manage.

Lewis showed that even this claim was suspect. Lewis won the first fall in twenty minutes. Lewis won the second fall in six minutes crushing Sampson in two straight falls.^{clxxxiv}

Promoters then booked Lewis into a rematch with Yussuf Hussane on Tuesday, August 18, 1914. Lewis and Hussane wrestled in front of a large crowd at the Broad Street Ball Park in Richmond.

Figure 31-Lewis vs. Hussane in Richmond, Virginia on Tuesday, August 18, 1914

Lewis won the first fall from Hussane with a double arm and scissors hold combination in forty-five minutes. Hussane took the second fall with an arm scissors and arm lock in twenty-six minutes. Lewis won the third fall and match with a head and arm lock in nineteen minutes, fifty seconds.[clxxxv] Fans heartily cheered Lewis, who the fans adopted as a local favorite.

On Thursday, August 27, 1914, Lewis wrestled "Honest John" Perrelli at the Roanoke Fairgrounds. The men wrestled two-out-of-three-falls. Lewis could use the stranglehold.

Perrelli enjoined early success using a half-Nelson and leg scissors combination to pin Lewis in six minutes to take the first fall. After the first fall, rain, the bane of outdoor sporting events, interfered with the match.[clxxxvi]

The rain made holds hard to apply and for both wrestlers to keep their feet. After twenty-seven minutes and fifteen seconds, Lewis won the second fall with the stranglehold.

Lewis won the third fall and match with a stranglehold at sixteen minutes, forty-six seconds. Due to the rainy conditions, Lewis agreed to wrestle Perrelli again on the following Monday, August 31, 1914.[clxxxvii]

Perrelli was not as competitive during the second match. Billy Sandow, who was managing Dr. Benjamin Roller, Lewis' opponent for Thursday, September 3, 1914, sat at ringside.

Lewis pinned Perrelli with an arm bar and scissors hold. Fans yelled at referee Bob Williams that Lewis did not hold Perrelli down long enough. However, Sandow agreed with the referee which quelled the controversy.[clxxxviii]

Perrelli looked exhausted to start the second fall. Lewis used a leg and body lock to pin Perrelli for the second fall in twenty-three minutes. Lewis beat Perrelli in straight falls. Lewis looked great leading into his rematch with Dr. Benjamin F. Roller.

Lewis wrestled Roller in front of a large crowd at Richmond, Virginia's Broad Street Ball Park. Lewis and Roller agreed to allow all holds after Lewis insisted on banning the toe hold if Roller insisted on banning the stranglehold.

The men wrestled defensively for the first twenty minutes with little action. Lewis finally took Roller to the ground and secured a near fall. Roller executed a head spin to escape the position and get back to his feet.

After forty minutes of wrestling, Roller used a half-Nelson and crotch hold to pin Lewis for the first fall.[clxxxix] Despite scoring the first fall, Roller looked more fatigued than Lewis entering the second fall.

The men rested eighteen minutes between the first and second falls. Lewis and Roller continued their defensive wrestling in the second fall until Lewis secured his first stranglehold at the six-minute mark.

Lewis had Roller in deep trouble but could not finish Roller with the stranglehold. After Roller broke two strangleholds, Lewis secured a leg scissors on Roller's neck and forced Roller to tap to the leg strangle.^{cxc}

After another fifteen minutes rest, the men started the third fall. Lewis pursued the stranglehold as Roller tried to defend against Lewis' attempts.

While trying to escape from Lewis' stranglehold, Roller ran into the upright that held up the lights. The impact of Roller hitting the post broke the wooden upright in half. The board knocked Roller insensible. Lewis fell on top of Roller for the third fall and match.^{cxci}

It took ten minutes for Dr. Roller to recover enough for his seconds to help him back to the dressing room. With such a fluke ending, the men were setting up a future rematch.

Dr. Roller defeated a Belgian wrestler named Gus Costello the following night in Roanoke. Lewis refereed the match between Roller and Costello.

On Monday, September 14, 1914, Lewis also wrestled Costello in Richmond's Broad Street Ball Park. Costello did not put Lewis in any danger during the match.

Lewis used an arm roll to pin Costello for the first fall at thirty-three minutes. Lewis took the second fall and match with a wristlock in thirty-seven minutes.[cxcii]

Lewis had an inactive September 1914 but would return to an active schedule in October. Lewis also had a new manager, but Lewis did not reveal this fact for three more months.

Figure 32- Lewis vs. Roller Advertisement (Public Domain)

Chapter 12 – Revealing the New Manager

Lewis opened October 1914 by accepting a match against Harry Faust, who tried taking liberties with Lewis in spring 1913. After accepting the Faust match, Lewis also agreed to wrestle "Farmer" James in Norfolk, Virginia's Pickwick Hall.

Lewis did not wrestle his first match in October until Monday, October 19, 1914. Lewis defeated James easily in a boring match. Lewis used a toe hold to take the first fall in forty-five minutes.

The hold injured James, who Lewis pinned in three minutes for the second fall and match. The Norfolk fans booed the lackluster bout.

Local middleweight champion John Kilonis offered to wrestle Lewis in an impromptu match. Promoters hoped to avoid a disaster that would keep fans away for months.

Lewis agreed and the men wrestled to a fifteen-minute draw. Fans cheered the Lewis-Kilonis match and left the hall happy.[cxciii]

On Tuesday, October 20, 1914, Lewis wrestled Harry Faust at Roanoke, Virginia's Jefferson Theater. Faust proved he learned his lesson on shooting, or wrestling legitimately, with Lewis. Faust worked the match and did not try Lewis this time.

Faust won the first fall with a scissors hold. Lewis won the next two falls in thirty-seven minutes and thirty-three minutes with the stranglehold.[cxciv]

On Friday, October 30, 1914, Lewis again wrestled Faust at the Jefferson Theater. Lewis agreed not to use the stranglehold in this match. However, the match ended with the same result.

Faust won the first fall with a hammerlock and body scissors combination in forty-six minutes. Lewis used a toe hold to even the match up at thirty-six minutes of the second fall.

The first toe hold damaged Faust to the point that Lewis needed only three minutes to make Faust give up to a second toe hold. Faust told a reporter for the Roanoke Times, "I'm going away from this town and never come back!"cxcv

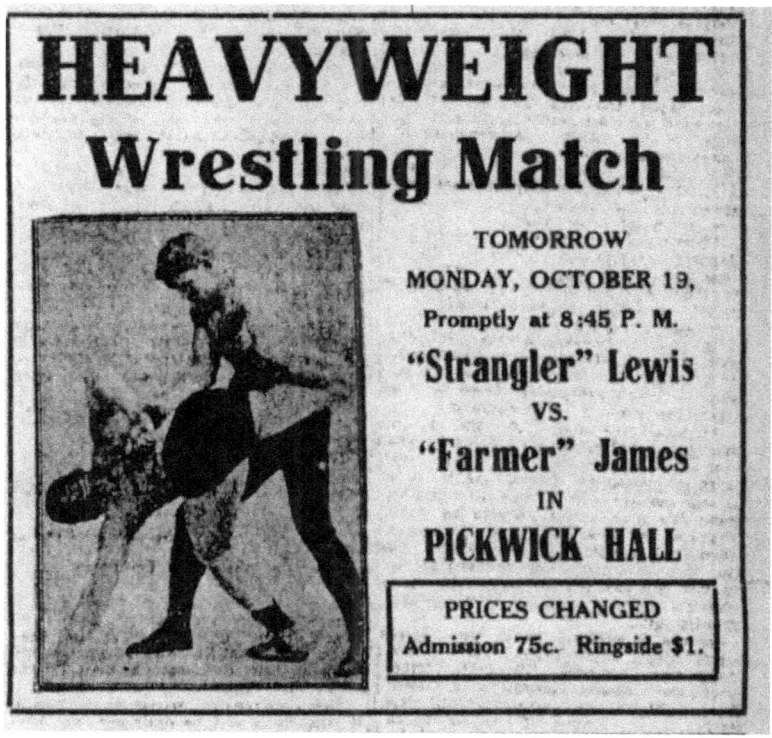

Figure 33-Advertisement for Ed "Strangler" Lewis vs. "Farmer" James (Public Domain)

In November 1914, Jerry Walls revealed that he no longer managed Ed

"Strangler" Lewis. Lewis left Walls at the end of the spring 1914 wrestling season in Kentucky.

Walls hoped to book Lewis against Walls' newest protégé Jack Stone.[cxcvi] Walls' revelation solved the mystery of why Lewis could never beat Stone when Walls managed Lewis.

The Roanoke promoters booked Lewis against Wladek Zbyszko on Monday, November 9, 1914, at the Jefferson Theater. Zbyszko claimed the title of American Heavyweight Wrestling Champion, but the title had evolved into more a promotional tactic than an actual title. Charlie Cutler, Dr. Benjamin Roller, and Wladek Zbyszko all claimed the title with little justification.

If the Virginia promoters were not aware of Lewis and Wladek Zbyszko's checkered history, Lewis and Zbyszko soon showed them. Lewis agreed not to use the stranglehold during the match.

Lewis and Zbyszko wrestled for sixty-five minutes, when Wladek Zbyszko butted Lewis in the stomach with his knee. Zbyszko's foul infuriated Lewis.

Lewis grabbed Zbyszko in a front face lock and started squeezing the stranglehold. Referee Joseph Hanna yelled for Lewis to break but Lewis ignored Hanna. Hanna warned Lewis three times to release the hold. Lewis refused leading Hanna to disqualify Lewis.

Hanna tried to pry Lewis off Wladek Zbyszko, but Hanna could not break Lewis' grip. Lewis finally released the hold. Zbyszko laid on the mat for minutes trying to recover from the stranglehold.

After the fans realized that Hanna disqualified Lewis, the fans booed the decision and yelled, "Fake. Fake." The Roanoke Times agreed that it would be difficult for promoters to stage future wrestling cards in Roanoke.[cxcvii]

Despite the fans threatening to riot, Hanna defended his decision to disqualify Lewis. Hanna said Zbyszko did provoke Lewis with his frequent fouls.

The odd thing about this match is that normally when Lewis started shooting in a match that started as a work Lewis punched the other wrestler in the face. In this match, Lewis hooked the other wrestler for the first time that I have seen. Lewis despised Wladek Zbyszko more than any other wrestler.

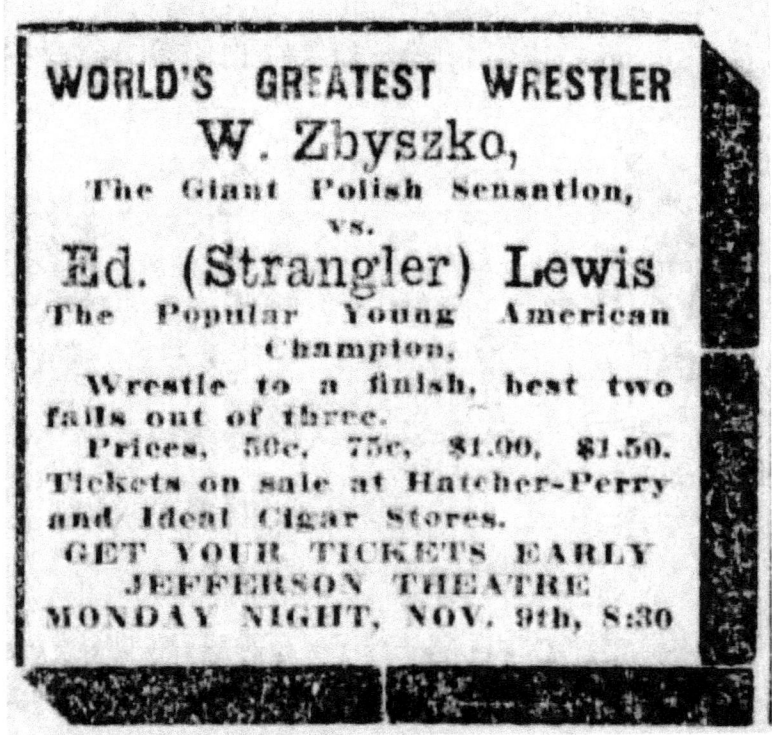

Figure 34-Ed "Strangler" Lewis vs. Wladek Zbyszko at the Jefferson Theater

Fan anger did not last long as a good crowd turned out to see Lewis wrestle Floyd Dormer the following Monday, November 16, 1914, at the Jefferson Theater. Lewis won this match in two straight falls.

Roanoke promoters were focused on another big opponent for Lewis. Promoters booked Lewis to wrestle a rematch with Dr. Benjamin Roller on December 7, 1914. The men agreed to wrestle for a purse of $800.00.[cxcviii]

What the fans in Roanoke did not know was that Roller defeated Lewis in Springfield, Massachusetts, on Wednesday, December 2, 1914. Lewis won the first fall before Roller took the next two falls.[cxcix] Local Virginia newspapers did not carry a story about the Springfield match, so the fans were none the wiser.

Promoters claimed Roller was defending the American Heavyweight Wrestling Championship. However, the championship did not really exist anymore. A handful of wrestlers claimed the title and ruined the lineage after 1913. The title disappears completely in 1922 but only existed as a promotional tactic between 1914-1922.[cc]

Lewis wrestled Roller at the Jefferson Theater on Monday, December 7th. This match played out like the Brattleboro match but with the results reversed.

Roller used a toe hold to defeat Lewis for the first fall in twenty-five minutes. Lewis used the stranglehold to take the second fall in forty-five minutes. Lewis took the third fall and match with a double arm wristlock.[cci] Roller claimed that he was still the American Heavyweight Wrestling Champion since Lewis used the stranglehold, a preposterous claim but it was professional wrestling.

On Thursday, December 17, 1914, Lewis wrestled Gus Kuvaris in Lynchburg, Virginia. Lewis wrestled Kuvaris at the

Academy of Music, which would play into the outcome.

Lewis won the first fall in thirty-seven minutes with a headlock. Lewis and Kuvaris were wrestling during the second fall, when Kuvaris fell from the stage into the orchestra pit.

Kuvaris tried to catch himself and dislocated his upper arm. The referee had to stop the match and award it to Lewis for Kuvaris' withdrawal.[ccii]

The following night, Friday, December 18th, Lewis wrestled Hjalmar Lundin at the Assembly Hall in Roanoke, Virginia. Lewis agreed not to use the stranglehold.

Lewis took the first fall in thirty-three minutes with the side roll. Lundin tied the match up with a wrist lock and body turn to take the second fall. Lewis won the third fall and match with a reverse body hold off Lundin's attempted body slam.[cciii]

Heading into January 1915 Lewis rode an impressive winning streak. Part of the reason behind his newfound success was revealed at the beginning of the new year. Billy Sandow had been managing Lewis for the past four months.[cciv]

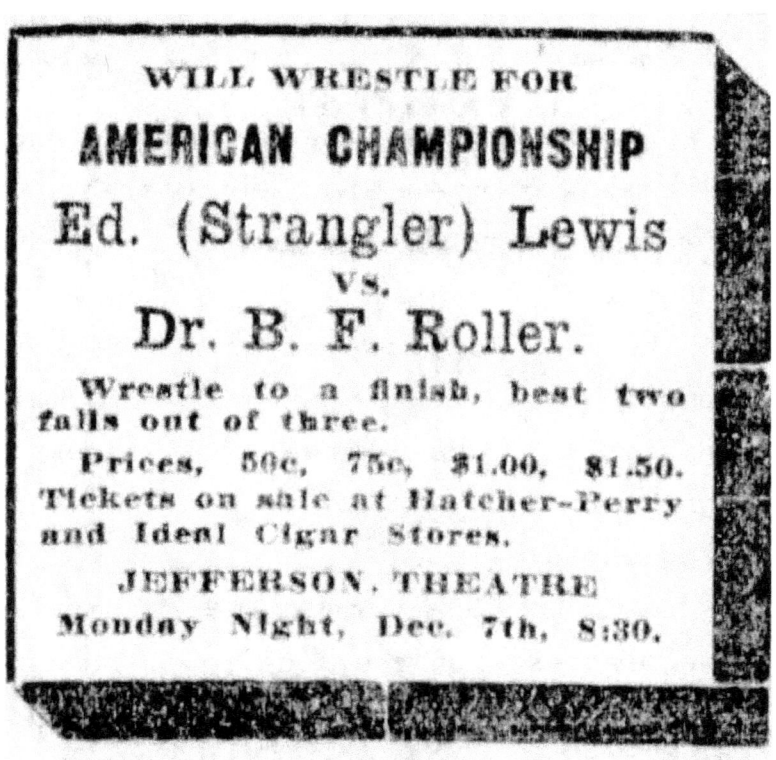

Figure 35- Lewis vs. Roller in Roanoke, Virginia during December 1914

Chapter 13 – Working with Billy Sandow

Lewis missed a match with Peter Karinoff in Roanoke, Virginia on January 18, 1915. Lewis wired the promoters that he could not get to Roanoke. Winter weather often threatened sporting events in December, January, and February.

On January 26, 1915, W.O. Yaeger, the former referee and new promoter in Lexington for the Kentucky Athletic Club, announced that he booked a match between Ed "Strangler" Lewis and Charlie Cutler for Tuesday, February 2, 1915. Yaeger printed a letter from Billy Sandow in announcing the match.

Sandow returned the contract for the match with a letter from promoters in Portland, who offered Sandow a $1,000.00 for the same match. Sandow said that he promised Yaeger the match, so Sandow returned the signed contract to Yaeger.

Sandow suggested that Yaeger contact the motion picture companies to film the match. Sandow and Yaeger would split the proceeds from the film companies.^{ccv}

Film companies filmed the biggest matches of the 1910s and 1920s including the second Frank Gotch vs George Hackenschmidt match on Labor Day 1911. Outside of twenty minutes of the two-hour match Joe Stecher and Earl Caddock wrestled in 1920, the film companies put the films in storage where the films rotted and were lost.

Lewis wrestled Cutler at the Ben Ali Theater in Lexington, Kentucky. Cutler claimed the American Heavyweight Wrestling Championship, the most claimed title in America.

The men rough housed for ten to fifteen minutes. Lewis rushed at Cutler, who was standing near the edge of the stage. Cutler side stepped Lewis as Cutler pushed Lewis from behind.

The momentum of Lewis' charge and Cutler's push sent Lewis over the footlights into the orchestra pit. The impact of the fall knocked Lewis unconscious.

Lewis could not continue. Normally, the referee W.O. Yaeger would award the match to Cutler, but Yaeger declared the match a draw. Yaeger said Cutler's push contributed to the end of the match.

Cutler agreed and accepted the draw. Billy Sandow took Lewis to the Good Samaritan Hospital, where the doctors admitted Lewis.[ccvi]

Despite Kentucky fans and newspaper reporters knowing Sandow managed Lewis, in Virginia, Chicago promoter Ed White fronted as Lewis' manager. In a situation you only find in professional wrestling, Lewis' actual manager Sandow accused Lewis of ducking the challenge of another Sandow wrestler, Peter Karinoff.[ccvii] Sandow hoped to build a big gate for the match between his wrestlers.

Sandow also shopped the match to W.O. Yaeger and the Kentucky Athletic Club. In Kentucky, M.W. Maxwell managed Karinoff for the official record.[ccviii]

Lewis agreed to wrestle Karinoff in Roanoke, Virginia on Tuesday, February 16, 1915.

Before this match on Wednesday, February 10, 1915, Lewis wrestled the "Italian Champion" Antonio Parina in Wheeling, West Virginia. Four hundred fans filed into the Market Auditorium to watch Lewis defeat Parina in two straight falls.

Parina used brute strength to avoid Lewis' offense. Parina appeared scared of Lewis and exerted nervous energy throughout the match. Parina exhausted himself quickly.

Lewis remained relaxed despite not being able to use the stranglehold. Lewis pinned Parina with a half-Nelson and body hold combination for the first fall.

Lewis used a half-Nelson and waist hold combination to pin Parina for the second fall and match following the fifteen-minute intermission. Reporters thought Lewis could have pinned Parina at any time despite Parina powering out of a couple of pin attempts.^{ccix}

Lewis continued his travels by wrestling Paul Martenson at Chicago's Haymarket Theater on Friday, February 12, 1915. Lewis won the match in two straight falls.

Lewis pinned Martenson with a head scissors and bar arm in thirty-five minutes, ten seconds. Lewis won the second fall and match with a cross bar arm in seventeen minutes.^{ccx}

On Saturday, February 13, 1915, Lewis wrestled Joe Geshtowt at the Chicago Athletic Association Arena. Lewis won the one fall match in fifteen minutes, ten seconds with a body scissors and wristlock.^{ccxi} Sandow kept Lewis on the hop in February bouncing between Kentucky, Illinois, Virginia, and West Virginia.

On Tuesday, February 16, 1915, Lewis returned to Roanoke, Virginia for a match with Peter Karinoff. The men wrestled at Roanoke's Academy of Music. Karinoff weighed two hundred seventy pounds to "Strangler" Lewis' two hundred twenty pounds.

Lewis wrestled Karinoff for fifteen minutes when Karinoff asked for a ten-minute rest after suffering a shoulder injury. Lewis was working a half-Nelson when Karinoff fell heavily on his shoulder.

Doctors examined Karinoff's shoulder. The doctors diagnosed a strained shoulder but no broken bones. Karinoff continued the match.

Lewis pinned Karinoff for the first fall in forty-two minutes, fifteen seconds with a body scissors and half-Nelson. After the intermission, Lewis used the same hold to pin Karinoff in eight minutes to take the match in straight falls.[ccxii]

On Thursday, February 18, 1915, Lewis wrestled Peter Roumainoff, who is Peter Karinoff. Both Roumainoff and Karinoff were the same size. 270-pound Russian wrestlers were not common in

American professional wrestling during the 1910s.

Figure 36- Lewis vs. Karinoff at the Academy of Music in Roanoke, Virginia during February 1915 (Public Domain)

The men wrestled at the Ben Ali Theater in Lexington, Kentucky. Lewis won this match in two straight falls as well.

Lewis won the first fall in thirty-nine minutes with a double arm bar. Lewis won the second fall in five minutes with the same hold.^{ccxiii}

The next night, Lewis was back in Chicago, Illinois in the co-main event underneath the Wladek Zbyszko vs. Mysterious Conductor match. Lewis won in two straight falls over Ilias Goverderela.

On Monday, February 22, 1915, Lewis wrestled frequent opponent Gus Kuvaris at the Market Auditorium in Wheeling, West Virginia. The newspapers carrying accounts of the match did not give an attendance figure.

Kuvaris won the first fall with a half-Nelson and scissors hold in one hour, four minutes, and thirty seconds. Lewis tied the match up after forty minutes, thirty seconds with a toe hold. Lewis won the third fall and match with a toe hold in seven minutes, thirty seconds.^{ccxiv}

With his victory over Kuvaris, Wheeling promoters announced that Lewis would wrestle Dr. Benjamin F. Roller in

March 1915. Jerry M. Walls also was trying to secure a match for his wrestler, Jack Stone, against Lewis.

On Friday, February 26, 1915, Lewis wrestled a rematch with Peter Karinoff. The men wrestled at Roanoke's Academy of Music. The match progressed like the past two matches between Lewis and Karinoff.

Lewis pinned Karinoff for the first fall in fifteen minutes, seventeen seconds with an arm lock and body scissors. Lewis won the second fall in two minutes, ten seconds with the same hold combination.[ccxv]

Karinoff told reporters that he made a mistake wrestling the rematch with Ed Lewis. Karinoff said his shoulder hurt so bad that Karinoff could not defend himself much less wrestle offensively.

Roanoke promoters announced another match between Lewis and Wladek Zbyszko in March 1915. Zbyszko would soon travel to New York in May 1915 to take part in the spring version of the 1915 New York International Wrestling Tournament.

Lewis wrestled his first match in March against Dr. Benjamin Roller at the Market Auditorium in Wheeling, West Virginia on Wednesday, March 3, 1915. The match drew two thousand fans to the auditorium a five-fold increase from the four hundred fans who turned out to see Lewis wrestle his first match in Wheeling.[ccxvi]

Figure 37- Dr. Benjamin Roller vs. Ed "Strangler" Lewis in Wheeling, West Virginia on March 3, 1915 (Public Domain)

Lewis and Roller wrestled back and forth for an hour before Lewis tossed Roller. The momentum of the fall took

Roller into the backstage wall. Roller fell to the floor.

Lewis flipped Roller to his back and pinned Roller for the first fall in one hour, six minutes.[ccxvii] After Lewis pinned Roller, the referee and Lewis realized Roller was unconscious.

The referee summonsed Drs. T. M. Haskins and E. B. Plant to examine Roller, who seconds helped back to the dressing room. Both physicians diagnosed a concussion.

Roller could not return to the mat within ten minutes as both Lewis and Roller agreed in the match stipulations. However, Lewis allowed the intermission to extend past the ten minutes.

Roller returned to the ring after twenty minutes. Dr. Haskins also went with Roller. Dr. Haskins told the referee that Roller could not continue.

Dr. Roller tried to protest but Dr. Haskins summoned a Wheeling Police Officer, who told the referee the match could not continue. The referee awarded

Lewis the match due to Roller's enforced withdrawal.[ccxviii]

Lewis traveled from Wheeling to Roanoke, Virginia for his next match against hated rival Wladek Zbyszko. Lewis wrestled Zbyszko at Roanoke's Academy of Music on Monday, March 8, 1915.

The men wrestled a boring two-hour draw. According to the rules of the match, the bout would be two-out-of-three-falls with a two-hour time limit.[ccxix] The match did not end with a fist fight so for a Lewis versus Zbyszko match it was a tame affair.

On Thursday, March 18, 1915, Lewis returned to Wheeling for a rematch with Dr. Roller. Lewis returned the favor from the earlier match Roller lost by dropping this match to Roller.

Lewis and Roller put on a fast match for the enjoyment of the fans. The men wrestled back and forth for an hour before Lewis tossed Roller over Lewis' head pinning Roller with an arm scissors and crotch hold.[ccxx]

Lewis and Roller continued the fast action during the second fall until the twenty-five-minute mark. Lewis held Roller in the air preparing to slam Roller to the mat. Roller shifted his weight causing both men to fall to the mat.

Roller landed on Lewis' ribs. Lewis was in obvious pain as Roller turned Lewis with a head and crotch hold.

Dr. Leach Cracraft examined Lewis. Dr. Cracraft said Lewis did not break any bones, but the fall badly bruised his ribs.[ccxxi]

Lewis returned to the mat in obvious pain. Roller took advantage of Lewis' weakened condition by applying a succession of toe holds. Lewis broke free of the holds though.

After twenty minutes of pressing Lewis, Roller used a scissors and half-Nelson combination to pin Lewis for the third fall and match.[ccxxii] Roller reclaimed the American Heavyweight Wrestling Championship after the match despite Charlie Cutler claiming the same title.

Lewis wrestled Ivan Michaeloff in Wheeling on Monday, March 29, 1915. Lewis wrestled in the co-main event of the card featuring Dr. Benjamin Roller vs. Illias Godervela.

Lewis won the match in two straight falls. Lewis won the first fall with a crotch hold in thirty-three minutes. Lewis won the second fall and match with a half-Nelson and further arm hold.[ccxxiii]

Billy Sandow promoted the Wheeling show. Either Dr. Roller or "Strangler" Lewis would wrestle Wladek Zbyszko, who was claiming the World Heavyweight Wrestling Championship, in April 1915.

According to Sandow, Wladek Zbyszko defeated his brother Stanislaus in Paris for the World Heavyweight Greco-Roman Wrestling Championship. Despite the preposterous explanation, Zbyszko claimed to be World Champion for a while until Zbyszko lost the 1915 New York International Wrestling Tournament.

Lewis was setup for further success. Sandow's management began to pay off in both the number of bookings for Lewis and the continued building of his national reputation. Eventually, Sandow and Lewis concocted a story about their partnership, which was as ridiculous and hyperbolic as their promotional tales to build a wrestling match.

Figure 38-Ivan Michaeloff circa 1915 (Public Domain)

Chapter 14 – Exploding the Myth about the Partnership

When researching professional wrestling, I find that the unbelievable or false stories about the wrestlers usually originate from the wrestlers themselves. Billy Sandow and Ed "Strangler" Lewis published the story of their partnership in a series of training course books in the 1920s.

While their version made for a delightful story, it did not have any basis in fact. In one of the books, *The Sandow-Lewis Library: Fundamentals of health, muscular development and wrestling*, the pair published their version of how they met.

The book claimed, "Just as the mention of the name of Ed " Strangler " Lewis calls to mind the name of Billy Sandow, so also does the mention of Billy Sandow's name call to mind the name of Ed "Strangler" Lewis. Billy Sandow, in his association with Ed "Strangler" Lewis, has been even more than Manager and Trainer; he has been a super-manager-a super-trainer, for the achievements shared by these two have no parallel in all athletic history. Recognizing in Lewis, the "amateur," the unmistakable natural qualifications of a great champion if properly developed and guided, Sandow was quick to persuade Lewis, the beginning wrestler, to become Lewis, the professional. Nor was Lewis any less quick to recognize in Sandow the particular abilities and certainty of purpose which mark the really great manager-trainer. Thus, from the earliest moment of their meeting , the association of Lewis and Sandow was a definite reality, and it has grown into so ideal a combination of Manager-Trainer and Champion that today this association is pointed out in the world of sport as no less remarkable than the very achievements to which it has led. Based upon perfect mutual understanding and respect, this partnership has endured and is often referred to as a model association of its kind. The intense study given by Billy Sandow to the perfection of training methods, and the outstanding success of Ed "Strangler" Lewis as an example of what those methods can do, demonstrates conclusively the vital part played by Billy Sandow in the achievements of this amazing combination of Manager-Trainer and World's Champion. Just as Lewis is frank in admitting the tremendous importance, in his success, of the tireless guidance received from Billy Sandow, the master physical culturist and manager-trainer is frank in admitting the equally great importance of Ed "Strangler" Lewis in their winning combination. "Nobody," says Billy Sandow," can doubt that we have worked hard for the success that has come to us, and we work equally hard to maintain our standing at the top in the wrestling world. Nothing has ever given me more pleasure than the splendid tribute paid to Ed "Strangler" Lewis by the widely known writer, Alfred W. McCann. Over the Champion's modest protest, I have insisted that this tribute be included in Volume Three of the Sandow - Lewis Library."

McCann wrote, "ED "STRANGLER" LEWIS And His Career Under the Management of Billy Sandow. To the public, the name of Ed " Strangler " Lewis implies, together with the name of Billy Sandow, a marvel of the world of sport. It is impossible to mention one without mentioning the other in the same breath, for the triumphs of Ed "Strangler" Lewis in his victorious progress to the heights of World's Champion Heavyweight Wrestler are equally shared by Billy Sandow, his manager and trainer; the man whose tireless energy combined with that of Ed "Strangler" Lewis to make their position in the wrestling world supreme . The record of Ed "Strangler" Lewis as the World's Heavyweight Wrestling Champion overshadows the records of all previous holders of that title, according to the expressed opinions of scores of authorities, and according to the actual and unmagnified tally of conquests the Champion has to his credit. The partnership of Ed "Strangler" Lewis and Billy Sandow has been a singularly happy one, even when considered from a practical business viewpoint alone. Theirs has been a policy of harmony and cooperation toward the single purpose of winning and maintaining the supreme position in the field of wrestling; and from that purpose they have never faltered, and they have not failed. The part of Lewis in this ideal partnership has been one of the resolute giving of his very best. Under the guidance of Billy Sandow, he has developed into the outstanding athlete of all wrestling history, for Sandow, too, has given of his very best to the end that Lewis should develop into that for which his natural qualifications, under proper handling, destined him. In the words of

Ed "Strangler" Lewis, himself, there is proof positive of the ideal combination that the association of the Champion and his Manager-Trainer has always been-no statement more eloquent of the unselfishness of their association could possibly be made: "All my strength, health and success, "Lewis has said," I owe to Billy Sandow and his methods."[ccxxiv]

As you can see, Sandow and Lewis included fiction along with fact in this account of their partnership. Sandow did manage Lewis into being the biggest star in professional wrestling. Their partnership made both men wealthy.

However, Sandow never knew Lewis as an amateur wrestler. Lewis had been wrestling professionally for at least three years before Sandow met Lewis in the fall of 1913.

It took another year for Lewis to leave the management of Jerry Walls and take Sandow up on his offer to manage him. Lewis did achieve much more success under Sandow than he did under Walls.

Part of the reason for this fiction was to sell their training courses to the public. Just as with their professional wrestling, Sandow and Lewis mixed fact with fiction to sell the public on what they were offering.

I am not inferring that Sandow was not important to Lewis' development or that Lewis could have gotten to where he did without Sandow. Sandow played a critical role in Lewis' development as a national level wrestler.

Lewis was critical in Sandow's development into one of the most powerful managers and promoters in professional wrestling. The true story of their partnership is compelling. However, they still juiced it up with tall tales and hyperbole.

In December 1915, Lewis joined the fall version of the 1915 New York International Wrestling Tournament. Lewis' entry into the tournament cemented him as a national wrestler. Before joining the tournament, Lewis and Sandow had six more months to cement their partnership.

Figure 39- Ed "Strangler" Lewis circa 1915

Chapter 15 – Trying to Stay Busy

Lewis pursued another match with Wladek Zbyszko, who was still making dubious claims to be the World Heavyweight Wrestling Championship. However, the 1915 New York International Wrestling Tournament scuttled these plans at least for a little while.

W.O. Yaeger of the Kentucky Athletic Club thought he secured a match between Lewis and Zbyszko for April 30, 1915. Zbyszko could have wrestled the match as the tournament did not start until the third week of May 1915.

However, Zbyszko backed out of the match at the last minute. Yaeger substituted Frank Hockman, "the German Oak," for Zbyszko.[ccxxv]

Prior to wrestling Hockman, Lewis defeated a wrestler named Karsten, who claimed to be the "Ohio Champion," in two straight falls in Huntington, West Virginia.[ccxxvi] Sixty wrestlers made up the 1915 New York International Tournament including Dr. Benjamin Roller and Wladek Zbyszko. Sandow would find available wrestlers harder to find because of the tournament.

A small crowd watched Lewis wrestle Hockman at the Ben Ali Theater in Lexington, Kentucky on Friday, April 30, 1915. Lewis toyed with the inferior wrestler before pinning Hockman in thirty-one minutes for the first fall.

Lewis needed only seventeen more minutes to defeat Hockman in straight falls.[ccxxvii] Yaeger realized that he might be losing the Lexington audience. To try to revive interest, Yaeger announced Lewis would wrestle Charlie Cutler, one of the claimants of the American Heavyweight Wrestling Championship.

West Virginia promoters booked a match between Ed "Strangler" Lewis and Dr. Benjamin Roller for Thursday, May 6, 1915. The men wrestled at the Auditorium in Wheeling, West Virginia.

Sandow and the West Virigina promoters were fortunate to book Dr.

Roller before the New York International Wrestling Tournament. Roller would not be able to wrestle outside of New York in a couple of weeks.

The wrestlers arrived at the arena late. Dr. Roller arrived first, so West Virginia promoter "Doc" Crane asked Roller to show wrestling holds to the crowd.

Roller showed holds for thirty minutes as the crowd enjoyed the exhibition. While Roller displayed his knowledge of wrestling, Crane secured a referee as regular referee George Phillips could not make it. Crane appointed Arch McFarland to referee.

Lewis and Roller entered the mat area around 9:40 p.m. Lewis weighed two hundred thirty pounds which was ten pounds heavier than Dr. Roller.[ccxxviii]

Lewis pressed the offense for the first fall. After forty-seven minutes, Lewis applied a waist hold and pinned Roller for the first fall.

After a ten-minute rest, Roller surprised Lewis with a crotch hold and pinned Lewis in one minute, thirty seconds. Lewis smiled, acknowledge Roller, and stayed in the ring during the intermission.

Lewis pressed the offense from the start. After chasing Roller for a couple of minutes, Lewis applied a scissors and hand hold. Roller tried to escape but Lewis held fast. Lewis pinned Roller in thirteen minutes.[ccxxix] Lewis won the third fall and match.

Wladek Zbyszko wired "Doc" Barnes that Zbyszko would wrestle either Lewis or Roller in a finish match for a purse of $1,200. Time would tell if the match came off after Zbyszko's earlier cancellation.

Lewis did not have long to rest after his victory over Roller. Lewis was due to wrestle Charlie Cutler at the Opera House in Lexington, Kentucky on Monday, May 10, 1915. It would be the first time Lewis wrestled Cutler since

Lewis went over the footlights and could not continue their match.

Figure 40- Dr. Benjamin F. Roller circa 1915 (Public Domain)

Prior to wrestling Lewis, Cutler wrestled Yussuf "Young" Hussane in Louisville, Kentucky on Friday, May 7, 1915. Lewis attended the match, which Cutler won handily. Lewis told newspaper reporters that he was able to scout Cutler and picked up tips for their match.[ccxxx]

Figure 41- Advertisement for Cutler vs. Lewis (Public Domain)

Heading into the match, Lewis was not going to defeat Charles Cutler. Martin "Farmer" Burns booked Cutler to wrestle Joe Stecher in the summer of 1915. Burns arranged for Cutler to lose to Stecher. Stecher would then claim the American Heavyweight Wrestling Championship and challenge Frank Gotch.

Gotch intended to lose to Stecher as well cementing Stecher as Gotch's successor as World Heavyweight Wrestling Champion. However, Gotch broke his ankle during training canceling Stecher vs. Gotch. The fans accepted Joe Stecher as World Champion anyway.[ccxxxi]

Since Cutler could not lose, Sandow and Lewis needed to produce a creative finish. However, the finish may have led to a legitimate fight between Lewis and Cutler.

Lewis and Cutler wrestled for one hour, fifteen minutes without either wrestler scoring an advantage. Cutler grabbed a front face lock, which Sandow screamed was a stranglehold.

W.O. Yaeger, who served as referee, said it was not a stranglehold despite Sandow's protest. Lewis finally freed himself and punched Cutler in the face twice.

Cutler fell to the mat stunned as Lewis jumped on the prone Cutler. While Lewis tried to punch Cutler again, Yaeger drug Lewis away from Cutler.

Cutler sat on the mat looking surprised as Sandow yelled at Yaeger that Yaeger should disqualify Cutler. Instead Yaeger disqualified Lewis for punching Cutler in the face.

Sandow and Lewis returned to the dressing room. Cutler followed minutes later.

Cutler screamed at Lewis as Cutler entered the dressing room area. Cutler tried to rush Lewis, but Lexington Police and Kentucky Athletic Club personnel kept them separated. The Lexington Police had to keep the fans out of the dressing room as word spread that Cutler and Lewis were continuing the fist fight.[ccxxxii]

Even though Lewis often punched his opponents when Lewis shot on them, Lewis used the punches to end the Cutler match to preserve Cutler's title. Cutler may have thought Lewis hit him too hard so the dressing room punch up could have been legitimate. Only Cutler, Lewis, and maybe Sandow, knew for sure.

The series takes an ironic turn two nights later. Cutler's brother Marty boxed professionally before taking up professional wrestling. On Wednesday, May 12th, in Huntington, West Virginia, Marty Cutler wrestled Ed "Strangler" Lewis. The match turned out to be close to a boxer versus wrestler match.

Lewis frustrated the less experienced Marty Cutler who often jabbed at Lewis' face. The referee should have disqualified Cutler, but Lewis waved the referee off.

Lewis slapped Cutler's punches away. Cutler occasionally landed a punch on Lewis but could not hurt Lewis. Lewis won the match in straight falls in twenty-five minutes and eighteen minutes.^{ccxxxiii}

On Friday, May 14, 1915, Lewis finally got his match with Wladek Zbyszko despite the New York International Tournament starting a week later. Zbyszko could not pass up Sandow's $1,200 purse for a match.

Lewis wrestled Zbyszko at the Market Auditorium in Wheeling, West Virginia. Zbyszko still claimed the World Championship, an increasingly dubious claim with the rise of Joe Stecher.

Zbyszko and Lewis pushed each other around the mat for the first hour and five minutes. Zbyszko consistently palm struck and butted Lewis. Lewis finally punched Zbyszko.^{ccxxxiv}

Zbyszko started punching Lewis and a slugfest ensued until the referee, managers and promoter separated the men. Promoter "Doc" Barnes ordered a ten-minute intermission and then said the men would continue wrestling.

The referee Karl Stens restarted the match. The men wrestled for about ten minutes before Zbyszko punched Lewis. Lewis started swinging too, which caused another brawl. Stens disqualified Zbyszko to end the match.[ccxxxv]

Sandow claimed Lewis won the world championship, but no one took the claim seriously. By the end of summer, the fans and sports reporters recognized Joe Stecher as the World Heavyweight Wrestling Champion.

Lewis wrestled the Virginia Champion Lou Witten in Huntington, West Virginia on Wednesday, May 26, 1915. Lewis beat Whitten in two straight falls in twenty-four minutes total.[ccxxxvi]

Lewis wanted another match with Zbyszko, but accepted a match in Lexington, Kentucky with Yussuf "Young" Hussane. Lewis wrestled Hussane at the Lexington Opera House on Friday, May 28, 1915.

Figure 42-Wladek Zbyszko circa 1915 (Public Domain)

The match disappointed the fans. Lewis pinned Hussane after thirty-six minutes of the first fall. After the intermission, Lewis and Hussane started shooting as the contest became a boring headbutting contest on the part of Hussane.

At one point, Billy Sandow yelled to Lewis, "Punch his eyes out!" A Lexington Police Officer escorted Sandow to the dressing room after this comment.

After an hour and five minutes of Hussane butting Lewis, the same Lexington Police Officer ordered the match stopped. Yaeger announced Lewis as the winner. The fans furiously demanded their money back. Instead, Yaeger announced the match was the last of the season due to the hot weather.[ccxxxvii]

In June 1915, Lewis returned how to Nekoosa, Wisconsin to see his parents. Lewis was home for two weeks before Charles Cutler sent him a telegram asking Lewis to help train Cutler for his match with Joe Stecher.[ccxxxviii]

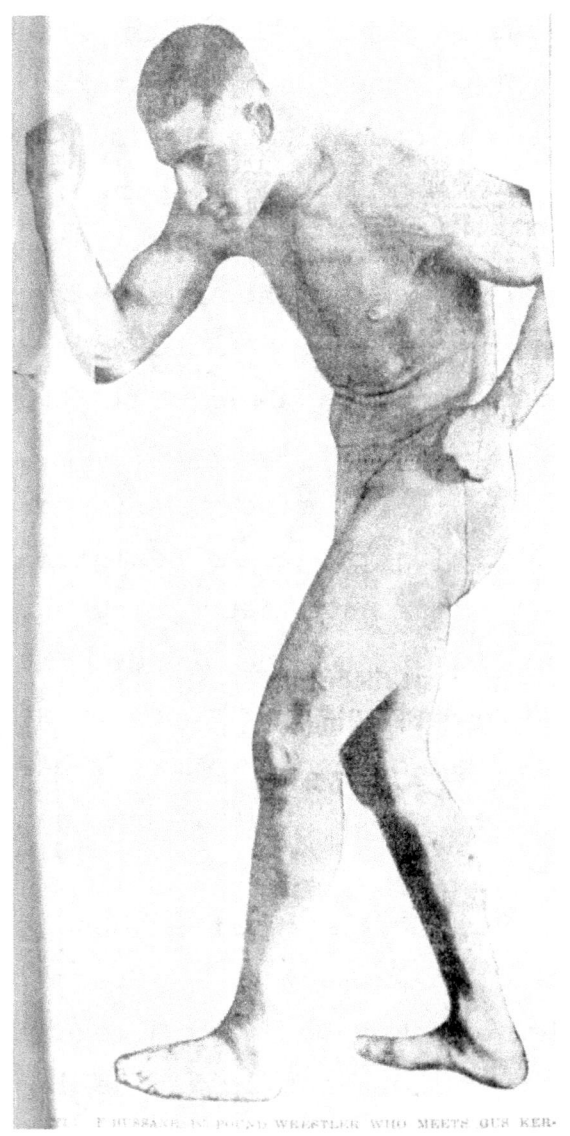

Figure 43- Yussuf Hussane in 1915 (Public Domain)

Lewis traveled with Stecher to Omaha, Nebraska, where Cutler continued training for the match with Joe Stecher. Stecher appeared as Lewis' greatest rival over the next fifteen years, but Lewis did not know Stecher prior to Stecher wrestling Cutler.

While Lewis trained with Cutler, the *Omaha Daily News* printed a claim Lewis often made but which had no basis in fact. Lewis claimed to be a graduate of the University of Kentucky.[ccxxxix] While Lewis did train the wrestling team at the university in Lexington, Kentucky, Lewis did not attend college.

Lewis wrestled professionally from the age of nineteen. Lewis did not arrive in Kentucky until 1913, when Lewis was twenty-two years old.

Lewis challenged Stecher to a match after Stecher beat Cutler, but Stecher declined. Sandow and Lewis could not raise a $500.00 side bet at the time.[ccxl]

Sandow issued a challenge to all the top wrestlers in the United States during August 1915.[ccxli]

Lewis and Sandow found matches difficult to come by in the summer of 1915. The wrestlers not engaged in the Stecher vs. Cutler match took part in the 1915 New York International Wrestling Tournament. Eventually, Lewis joined the tournament but not until the end of fall 1915.

Figure 44- Ed "Strangler" Lewis circa 1915 (Public Domain)

Chapter 16 — Fall 1915

Ed "Strangler" Lewis found himself in Indiana during September 1915. Billy Sandow discovered in Indiana a welcome venue for his top wrestler.

Sandow made headlines in Indiana before Lewis even arrived. Sandow cornered Yussuf Hussane in the offices of the *Evansville Courier*, where wrestlers were negotiating with the local promoter.

Sandow asked Hussane why Hussane kept backing out of Sandow's attempts to match Hussane with "Strangler" Lewis. Hussane said he was not interested in another match with Lewis.

Sandow responded by punching Hussane in the jaw. Sandow followed up with a kick to the groin, but the kick missed and hit Hussane in the hip.

Hussane stood up and threw a punch at Sandow, which missed. After recovering from the first shock, wrestlers Phil Veatch and William Demetral broke up the fight.

Sandow called Hussane a coward. Sandow said if he could not arrange a match for Lewis with Hussane, Demetral, or Roller, Sandow would book Lewis against Ivan Linow.[ccxlii]

Usually, wrestlers fought outside the arena to generate fan interest in their grudge wrestling match. It was not usually for the manager to beat up his wrestler's opponent. If lightweight wrestler Billy Sandow can beat up Hussane, why would fans pay to see him wrestle the more formidable Ed "Strangler" Lewis.

While Sandow negotiated for Lewis, Lewis was training on a farm in Lansing, Iowa. Lewis expressed his fervent desire to get back to wrestling.

Sandow also wanted to secure a match for Lewis with Dr. Roller. However, Roller told newspapers that Lewis had no claim to the American Heavyweight Wrestling Championship as Roller was still champion.

Fans and sports reporters recognized Joe Stecher as the American Heavyweight Wrestling Champion. After Gotch's training accident in July 1915, Gotch pulled out of the match with Stecher. Fans then recognized Stecher as World Heavyweight Wrestling Champion.

Still, Roller and Lewis claimed the non-existent championship. If Lewis wanted to wrestle Roller, Sandow needed to arrange the match quickly. Roller would be heading back to New York for the fall version of the 1915 New York International Wrestling Tournament.

On Wednesday, September 8, 1915, Lewis arrived in Evansville, Indiana. The day before Yussuf Hussane heard Lewis was traveling to Evansville. The news caused Hussane to suddenly leave Evansville.[ccxliii]

Hussane did not tell Promoter William H. Barton, the former promoter for Lexington, Kentucky, that he was leaving. Hussane claimed he was not avoiding Lewis but no one believed Hussane's story.

Promoter Barton worked with Sandow to arrange a match between Lewis and Sulo Hevonpaa, a Finnish wrestler. Hevonpaa featured prominently in the spring version of the 1915 New York International Wrestling Tournament. Hevonpaa would appear in silent films as well as Broadway productions in the 1920s and 1930s.

Lewis wrestled Hevonpaa at the Wells Bijou Theater in Evansville, Indiana on Friday, September 17, 1915. Lewis had little trouble with Hevonpaa defeating Hevonpaa in sixteen and twenty-four minutes, respectively.[ccxliv] Because of the intense heat, Lewis did not push the pace too hard.

In Evansville, the wrestlers wrestled in a ring. Prior to his time in Indiana, Lewis wrestled on mats placed on a stage.

Figure 45- Sulo Hevonpaa (Public Domain)

In one of the comedic moments of the match involving the ring, Hevonpaa lunged wildly at Lewis. Lewis dropped to the mat and Hevonpaa sailed through the ropes to the floor on the other side of the ring.[ccxlv]

After Lewis defeated Hevonpaa, Jess Westergaarde sent a challenge to Lewis through Billy Sandow. Westergaarde, one of Gotch's frequent training partner, wanted to stop Lewis' national momentum.

Sandow arranged for Lewis to wrestle Westergaarde on Thursday, September 30, 1915. However, Westergaarde backed out of the match.

Promoter Barton arranged for Bobby Managoff, Sr. to replace Westergaarde. However, Managoff did not arrive in Evansville in time to wrestle Lewis.

Barton quickly forgot about this development because Barton secured a match between Lewis and current World Heavyweight Champion Joe Stecher. This match was the first of three legitimate contests Lewis and Stecher wrestled.

On Friday, October 15, 1915, Lewis wrestled "Buck" Weaver in Mount Carmel, Illinois. Lewis defeated Weaver easily in two straight falls.^{ccxlvi}

The *Evansville Press* printed an advertisement for the Stecher versus Lewis match on Wednesday, October 22, 1915. Promoter Ed Barton charged five dollars for ringside and box seats, which normally sold for two dollars. In 2023 dollars, the ringside box seats would cost $150.00.

WORLD'S CHAMPIONSHIP WRESTLING MATCH
JOE STECHER (The Nebraska Wonder)
vs. ED. "STRANGLER" LEWIS
AT THE WELLS BIJOU THEATRE, WEDNESDAY NIGHT, OCT. 20th

PRICES:
Ringside and Boxes $5.00	Gallery (reserved) 1.50
Entire Lower Floor 3.00	General Admission 1.00
Balcony (first six rows) 2.50	Money orders and certified checks must
Balcony (balance) 2.00	be payable to Treasurer, Wells Bijou

Figure 46-Advertisement for the Stecher vs. Lewis match in Evansville during 1915 with prices listed (Public Domain)

Barton also billed Lewis as American Heavyweight Champion although Lewis did not have a legitimate claim to the title.

Barton sold three thousand dollars in tickets before the day of the big match.ccxlvii Barton expected a five thousand dollar gate after adding in the walk-up customers on the day of the event.

Stecher feared fans mobbing him, so he stayed in Vincennes, Indiana. Stecher only arrived in Evansville on the night of Tuesday, October 19, 1915.

Stecher also received a telegram warning him about a potential double-cross. Stecher's brother and manager Tony Stecher spoke with referee Sisson. The referee assured the Stechers that he would not be party to any double-crosses.ccxlviii

An unknown party also sent Mayor Bosse a telegram to "stop the fake wrestling match." Despite Lewis and Stecher wrestling the match legitimately, the outcome of the match added to the mayor's doubts.

The match unfolded as most legitimate contests between equally matched competitors. Lewis and Stecher pushed each other around the ring for two hours and three minutes.

Stecher never took Lewis down. Lewis only took Stecher to the mat four times but released Stecher each time Stecher tried to use a toe hook on Lewis. Stecher used the toe hook to setup the leg scissors. Lewis wanted no part of the hold.[ccxlix]

Stecher told Sisson that Lewis had to try to wrestle. Lewis and Sandow insisted that Gotch used the same strategy to defeat Georg Hackenschmidt in their first match. Lewis continued to wrestle defensively.

Tired of Lewis' excessively defensive wrestling style, Stecher shoved Lewis, who fell through the ropes. Lewis claimed to have hit his head on the way down. Lewis complained that he could not continue.

Dr. Phil Warter examined Lewis and said Lewis was not too injured. Sandow objected, so Drs. Greenleaf and Louis

Fritsch examined Lewis. Both physicians agreed with Dr. Warter's diagnosis.[ccl]

Despite the three doctor's opinions, Lewis refused to continue. Referee Sisson awarded Stecher the first fall. Sisson said if Lewis could not continue after the ten-minute intermission, Sisson would award the match to Stecher.

Mayor Bosse also said that Lewis should continue since the doctors said that Lewis could continue. After ten minutes, Lewis did not return to the ring. Sisson awarded the match to Stecher.[ccli]

Mayor Bosse and Chief of Police Ed Schmidt confiscated part of the gate receipts. Mayor Bosse said he believed the match to be a fake. Bosse was going to give part of the money to charity. Bosse said Lewis and Stecher only deserved the normal ticket price gate receipts.[cclii]

Mayor Bosse took money that he had no right to based on his false belief that the wrestlers faked or worked the match. Most people could not tell the difference between a worked exhibition or a legitimate contest.

Legitimate contests often ended in boring stalemates. Besides promotional control, wrestling evolved into a worked exhibition because worked matches entertained the fans.

Stecher told newspaper reporters that Lewis was the toughest wrestler he ever faced. The men wrestled two more legitimate contests before Lewis finally defeated his greatest in-ring rival.

Sandow and Tony Stecher tried to arrange for a rematch on Saturday, November 13, 1915, in Chicago, Illinois. However, Joe Stecher caught a virus, which cancelled the match. By the time Stecher was ready to get into the ring, Lewis already entered the fall version of the 1915 New York International Wrestling Tournament postponing their next contest until 1916.

Lewis finished the tournament as the third highest rated wrestler, but Lewis defeated every contestant in catch-as-catch-can wrestling during the tournament except for Aleksander "Alex" Aberg. Aberg, a Greco-Roman wrestling specialist, refused to wrestle Lewis under catch rules. Like every other wrestler in the tournament, Aberg defeated Lewis in a match under Greco-Roman wrestling rules.[ccliii]

After the tournament, Lewis was a national star. The farm boy from Nekoosa was one of the biggest stars in professional wrestling. Lewis was only getting warmed up.

Figure 47- Joe Stecher circa 1915 (Public Domain)

Conclusion

The year and a half that Ed "Strangler" Lewis spent in Kentucky set him up for his future national success. The presence of Bob Fredericks forced Lewis to change his name from Bob Friedrich to Ed "Strangler" Lewis. Lewis took the name in homage to fellow Wisconsin professional wrestler Evan "Strangler" Lewis.

Louisville promoter Jerry M. Walls, who managed Lewis for his eighteen months in Kentucky, also proved critical in building Lewis' reputation. Walls brought in other national stars like William Demetral and Dr. Benjamin Roller to wrestle Lewis.

Walls also brought in Billy Jenkins, which brought Jenkin's manager Billy Sandow to Lexington. Sandow recognized Lewis' potential and recruited Lewis away from Walls.

Lewis taking on Sandow as a manager led to his transformation into the World Heavyweight Wrestling Champion. Lewis, Sandow, and Joseph "Toots" Mondt formed the Gold Dust Trio in late 1922. The Trio dominated professional wrestling during the 1920s making a fortune for all three men.

Without his time in Kentucky, Lewis would not have achieved these heights. Those eighteen months in Kentucky setup all his future success.

Figure 48- Ed Lewis in late 1915 (Public Domain)

Other Combat Sports Books by Ken Zimmerman Jr.

Wayfarer in a Foreign Land: Sorakichi Matsuda Wrestles in America

Shooting or Working? The History of the American Heavyweight Title

Gotch vs. Zbyszko: The Quest for Redemption

Double-Crossing the Gold Dust Trio: Stanislaus Zbyszko's Last Hurrah

Masked Marvel To The Rescue: The Gimmick That Saved the 1915 New York Wrestling Tournament

Gotch vs. Hackenschmidt: The Matches That Made and Destroyed Legitimate American Professional Wrestling

Evan "The Strangler" Lewis: The Most Feared Wrestler of the 19th Century

William Muldoon: The Solid Man Conquers Wrestling and Physical Culture

Morrissey vs. Poole: Politics, Prizefighting, and the Murder of Bill the Butcher

Bibliography

Newspapers

The Birmingham News (Birmingham, Alabama)

Brattleboro Reformer (Brattleboro, Vermont)

The Buffalo News (Buffalo, New York)

The Cairo Bulletin (Cairo, Illinois)

The Chicago Tribune (Chicago, Illinois)

The Courier-Journal (Louisville, Kentucky)

The Daily Republican-Register (Mount Carmel, Illinois)

The Daily Tribune (Wisconsin Rapids, Wisconsin)

The Evansville Courier and Press (Evansville, Indiana)

The Evansville Press (Evansville, Indiana)

The Herald News (Joliet, Illinois)

The Inter Ocean (Chicago, Illinois)

Ledger-Star (Norfolk, Virginia)

The Lexington Herald (Lexington, Kentucky)

The Lexington Herald-Ledger (Lexington, Kentucky)

The Licking Valley Courier (West Liberty, Kentucky)

The Macon News (Macon, Georgia)

The Omaha Daily News (Omaha, Nebraska)

The Omaha World-Herald (Omaha, Nebraska)

The Richmond Times-Dispatch (Richmond, Virginia)

The Roanoke Times (Roanoke, Virginia)

Vermont Phoenix (Brattleboro, Vermont)

The World-News (Roanoke, Virginia)

The Wheeling Intelligencer (Wheeling, West Virginia)

The Winchester Sun (Winchester, Kentucky)

The Wood County Reporter (Grand Rapids, Wisconsin)

Books

Gotch vs. Zbyszko: The Quest for Redemption by author

Masked Marvel To The Rescue: The Gimmick That Saved the 1915 New York Wrestling Tournament by the author

The Sandow-Lewis Library: Fundamentals of health, muscular development and wrestling by Billy Sandow and Ed "Strangler" Lewis

Shooting or Working? The History of the American Heavyweight Title by the author

Websites

www.wrestlingdata.com

www.newspapers.com

About the Author

Ken Zimmerman Jr. lives outside of St. Louis, Missouri. Ken has been interested in combat sports since watching professional wrestling from St. Louis in the late 1970s and his introduction to boxing by his stepdad, Ernest Charles Diaz, who raised him. A lifelong martial artist, Ken holds rank in three martial arts including a 4th Degree black belt in Taekwondo.

If you like this book, you can sign up for Ken's newsletter to receive information about future book releases. You can sign up for the newsletter and receive a bonus e-book at www.kenzimmermanjr.com.

Endnotes

Chapter 1
[i] The Daily Tribune (Wisconsin Rapids, Wisconsin), December 28, 1910, p. 4
[ii] The Daily Tribune, March 1, 1911, p. 4
[iii] The Cairo Bulletin, January 19, 1911, p. 2
[iv] Vermont Phoenix, July 19, 1912, p. 6
[v] Vermont Phoenix, July 26, 1912, p. 4

Chapter 2
[vi] The Courier-Journal, January 25, 1913, p. 10
[vii] Ibid
[viii] Ibid
[ix] The Journal-Courier, February 1, 1913, p. 11
[x] Ibid
[xi] The Lexington Herald, February 7, 1913, p. 3
[xii] The Lexington Herald, February 12, 1913, p. 12
[xiii] The Lexington Herald, February 15, 1913, p. 12
[xiv] The Lexington Herald, February 18, 1913, p. 3
[xv] The Lexington Herald, February 20, 1913, p. 5

Chapter 3
[xvi] The Lexington Herald, February 23, 1913, p. 9
[xvii] The Lexington Herald, March 3, 1913, p. 3
[xviii] The Lexington Herald, March 7, 1913, p. 5
[xix] Ibid
[xx] The Courier-Journal, March 13, 1913, p. 8
[xxi] The Courier-Journal, March 15, 1913, p. 10
[xxii] Ibid
[xxiii] The Lexington Herald-Ledger, March 29, 1913, p. 3
[xxiv] Ibid
[xxv] Ibid
[xxvi] The Lexington Herald, April 9, 1913, p. 3
[xxvii][xxvii] Ibid
[xxviii] Ibid
[xxix] The Lexington Herald-Ledger, April 13, 1913, p. 7
[xxx] The Courier-Journal, April 19, 1913, p. 11
[xxxi] Ibid

[xxxii] The Lexington Herald, April 29, 1913, p. 12

Chapter 4
[xxxiii] The Lexington Hearld, May 1, 1913, p. 10
[xxxiv] The Lexington Herald, May 5, 1913, p. 3
[xxxv] The Lexington Herald, May 6, 1913, p. 12
[xxxvi] Ibid
[xxxvii] Ibid
[xxxviii] Ibid
[xxxix] The Lexington Herald, May 10, 1913, p.
[xl] Ibid
[xli] The Lexington Herald-Leader, May 8, 1913, p. 12
[xlii] Masked Marvel to the Rescue by author
[xliii] The Lexington Herald, May 15, 1913, p. 6
[xliv] Ibid
[xlv] Ibid
[xlvi] The Lexington Herald, May 22, 1913, p. 6
[xlvii] The Licking Valley Courier, May 29, 1913, p. 1
[xlviii] The Lexington Herald, June 6, 1913, p. 8
[xlix] Ibid
[l] The Lexington Herald, June 8, 1913, p. 2
[li] The Lexington Herald, June 18, 1913, p. 6
[lii] Ibid
[liii] Ibid
[liv] The Lexington Herald-Leader, June 26, 1913, p. 3
[lv] The Lexington Herald, July 1, 1913, p. 9
[lvi] The Lexington Herald, July 2, 1913, p. 5

Chapter 5
[lvii] The Lexington Herald-Ledger, September 10, 1913, p. 12
[lviii] The Lexington Herald-Ledger, September 11, 1913, p. 2
[lix] The Lexington Herald, September 13, 1913, p. 7
[lx] Ibid
[lxi] Ibid
[lxii] Ibid
[lxiii] The Lexington Herald-Ledger, September 14, 1913, p. 10
[lxiv] The Lexington Herald, September 16, 1913, p. 9
[lxv] The Lexington Herald-Leader, September 19, 1913, p. 2
[lxvi] Ibid
[lxvii] Ibid

[lxviii] The Courier-Journal, September 19, 1913, p. 9
[lxix] The Lexington Herald-Leader, September 21, 1913, p. 9
[lxx] The Courier-Journal, September 30, 1913, p. 9
[lxxi] Ibid
[lxxii] Ibid
[lxxiii] The Lexington Herald-Leader, September 30, 1913, p. 12

Chapter 6

[lxxiv] The Winchester Sun, October 8, 1913, p. 2
[lxxv] The Lexington Herald-Leader, October 14, 1913, p. 5
[lxxvi] The Winchester Sun, October 22, 1913, p. 3
[lxxvii] Ibid
[lxxviii] The Lexington Herald-Leader, October 22, 1913, p. 3
[lxxix] The Inter Ocean, November 5, 1913, p. 13.
[lxxx] Ibid
[lxxxi] The Herald News, November 6, 1913, p. 8
[lxxxii] The Lexington Herald-Leader, November 12, 1913, p. 2
[lxxxiii] The Lexington Herald-Leader, November 15, 1913, p. 4
[lxxxiv] Ibid
[lxxxv] The Chicago Tribune, November 16, 1913, p. 23
[lxxxvi] The Inter Ocean, November 18, 1913, p. 13
[lxxxvii] The Inter Ocean, November 21, 1913, p. 14
[lxxxviii] The Inter Ocean, November 22, 1913, p. 13
[lxxxix] The Lexington Herald, November 22, 1913, p. 8
[xc] The Inter Ocean, November 25, 1913, p. 13
[xci] Chicago Tribune, November 27, 1913, p. 12
[xcii] Ibid
[xciii] Ibid

Chapter 7

[xciv] Chicago Tribune, November 30, 1913, p. 24
[xcv] Ibid
[xcvi] The Lexington Herald, December 6, 1913, p. 6
[xcvii] Ibid
[xcviii] The Lexington Herald, December 10, 1913, p. 10
[xcix] The Lexington Herald, December 15, 1913, p. 6
[c] Ibid
[ci] Ibid
[cii] Ibid
[ciii] The Lexington Herald, December 20, 1913, p. 3

[civ] The Lexington Herald, December 26, 1913, p. 7
[cv] Ibid
[cvi] Ibid
[cvii] Ibid
[cviii] Gotch vs. Zbyszko: The Quest for Redemption by author

Chapter 8
[cix] The Lexington Herald, January 2, 1914, p. 7
[cx] The Lexington Herald-Leader, January 9, 1914, p. 2
[cxi] The Lexington Herald, January 10, 1914, p. 3
[cxii] Ibid
[cxiii] The Lexington Herald, January 13, 1914, p. 9
[cxiv] Ibid
[cxv] Ibid
[cxvi] The Lexington Herald-Leader, January 16, 1914, p. 2
[cxvii] The Lexington Herald, January 24, 1914, p. 12
[cxviii] Ibid
[cxix] Ibid
[cxx] Ibid
[cxxi] Ibid
[cxxii] The Lexington Herald, January 31, 1914, p. 3
[cxxiii] The Lexington Herald, February 4, 1914, p. 12
[cxxiv] Ibid
[cxxv] Ibid
[cxxvi] Ibid
[cxxvii] The Lexington Herald, February 6, 1914, p. 16
[cxxviii] Ibid
[cxxix] The Lexington Herald, February 7, 1914, p. 10
[cxxx] The Inter Ocean, February 10, 1914, p. 13
[cxxxi] The Lexington Herald, February 11, 1914, p. 12
[cxxxii] Ibid
[cxxxiii] Ibid
[cxxxiv] The Lexington Herald-Leader, February 19, 1914, p. 2
[cxxxv] Ibid
[cxxxvi] Ibid

Chapter 9
[cxxxvii] The Birmingham News, March 1, 1914, p. 13
[cxxxviii] The Birmingham News, March 2, 1914, p. 10
[cxxxix] The Birmingham News, March 3, 1914, p. 10

[cxl] The Birmingham News, March 7, 1914, p. 8
[cxli] Ibid
[cxlii] The Birmingham News, March 17, 1914, p. 10
[cxliii] Ibid
[cxliv] Ibid
[cxlv] The Lexington Herald-Leader, March 21, 1914, p. 5
[cxlvi] The Lexington Herald, March 24, 1914, p. 16
[cxlvii] Ibid
[cxlviii] Ibid
[cxlix] The Lexington Herald-Leader, March 31, 1914, p. 11

Chapter 10

[cl] The Macon News, April 2, 1914, p. 5
[cli] Ibid
[clii] The Lexington Herald-Leader, April 3, 1914, p. 11
[cliii] The Courier-Journal, April 4, 1914, p. 9
[cliv] The Courier-Journal, April 7, 1914, p. 7
[clv] The Lexington Herald-Leader, April 8, 1914, p. 1
[clvi] Ibid
[clvii] The Lexington Herald-Leader, April 11, 1914, p. 3
[clviii] The Buffalo News, April 24, 1914, p. 16
[clixclix] The Lexington Herald, April 28, 1914, p. 6
[clx] Ibid
[clxi] Ibid
[clxii] Ibid
[clxiii] The Macon News, May 8, 1914, p. 10
[clxiv] The Buffalo News, May 12, 1914, p. 14
[clxv] The Macon News, May 15, 1914, p. 5
[clxvi] Ibid
[clxvii] Ibid
[clxviii] The Macon News, May 20, 1914, p. 9
[clxix] The Macon News, May 22, 1914, p. 7
[clxx] Ibid
[clxxi] The Lexington Herald, May 30, 1914, p. 3
[clxxii] Ibid

Chapter 11

[clxxiii] The Lexington Herald, July 12, 1914, p. 7
[clxxiv] The Roanoke Times, July 10, 1914, p. 6
[clxxv] The Roanoke Times, July 18, 1914, p. 6

clxxvi Ibid
clxxvii The Richmond Times Dispatch, July 22, 1914, p. 7
clxxviii Ibid
clxxix Ledger-Star, July 23, 1914, p. 15
clxxx The Roanoke Times, July 28, 1914, p. 2
clxxxi Ibid
clxxxii The Roanoke Times, August 1, 1914, p. 2
clxxxiii Richmond Times-Dispatch, August 6, 1914, p. 6
clxxxiv Richmond Times-Dispatch, August 12, 1914, p. 7
clxxxv Richmond Times-Dispatch, August 19, 1914, p. 6
clxxxvi The Roanoke Times, August 28, 1914, p. 6
clxxxvii Ibid
clxxxviii The Roanoke Times, September 1, 1914, p. 6
clxxxix Richmond Times-Dispatch, September 4, 1914, p. 5
cxc Ibid
cxci Ibid
cxcii Richmond Times-Dispatch, September 15, 1914, p. 4

Chapter 12

cxciii Ledger-Star, October 20, 1914, p. 14
cxciv The World News, October 21, 1914, p. 9
cxcv The Roanoke Times, October 31, 1914, p. 2
cxcvi The Lexington Herald, October 11, 1914, p. 9
cxcvii The Roanoke Times, November 10, 1914, p. 1
cxcviii The Roanoke Times, December 1, 1914, p. 7
cxcix The Brattleboro Reformer, December 3, 1914, p. 3
cc Shooting or Working? The History of the American Heavyweight Wrestling Championship by author
cci The World-News, December 8, 1914, p. 7
ccii The Roanoke Times, December 18, 1914, p. 1
cciii The Roanoke Times, December 19, 1914, p. 5
cciv The Lexington Herald-Leader, January 3, 1915, p. 10

Chapter 13

ccv The Lexington Herald-Leader, January 26, 1915, p. 2
ccvi The Lexington Herald-Leader, February 3, 1915, pp. 2,6
ccvii The World-News, February 4, 1915, p. 2
ccviii The Lexington Herald-Leader, February 9, 1915, p. 2
ccix The Wheeling Intelligencer, February 11, 1915, p. 7
ccx Chicago Tribune, February 13, 1915, p. 9

[ccxi] Chicago Tribune, February 14, 1915, p. 24
[ccxii] The World-News, February 17, 1915, p. 9
[ccxiii] Lexington Herald-Leader, February 19, 1915, p. 2
[ccxiv] The Wheeling Intelligencer, February 23, 1915, p. 7
[ccxv] The World-News, February 27, 1915, p. 7
[ccxvi] The Wheeling Intelligencer, March 4, 1915, p. 7
[ccxvii] Ibid
[ccxviii] Ibid
[ccxix] The Roanoke Times, March 9, 1915, p. 7
[ccxx] The Wheeling Intelligencer, March 19, 1915, p. 12
[ccxxi] Ibid
[ccxxii] Ibid
[ccxxiii] The Wheeling Intelligencer, March 30, 1915, p. 7

Chapter 14
[ccxxiv] *The Sandow-Lewis Library: Fundamentals of health, muscular development and wrestling* by Billy Sandow and Ed "Strangler" Lewis

Chapter 15
[ccxxv] The Lexington Herald-Leader, April 26, 1915, p. 5
[ccxxvi] The Lexington Herald, April 30, 1915, p. 8
[ccxxvii] The Lexington Herald, May 1, 1915, p. 6
[ccxxviii] The Wheeling Intelligencer, May 7, 1915, p.7
[ccxxix] Ibid
[ccxxx] The Lexington Herald, May 9, 1915, p. 13
[ccxxxi] *Masked Marvel to the Rescue* by author
[ccxxxii] The Lexington Herald, May 11, 1915, p. 6
[ccxxxiii] The Lexington Herald-Leader, May 13, 1915, p. 3
[ccxxxiv] The Wheeling Intelligencer, May 15, 1915, p. 16
[ccxxxv] Ibid
[ccxxxvi] The Lexington Herald-Leader, May 27, 1915, p. 2
[ccxxxvii] The Lexington Herald, May 29, 1915, p. 9
[ccxxxviii] The Wood County Reporter, June 10, 1915, p. 1
[ccxxxix] The Omaha Daily News, July 5, 1915, p. 9
[ccxl] Ibid
[ccxli] The Omaha World-Herald, August 17, 1915, p. 8
[ccxlii] The Evansville Press, September 6, 1915, p. 6
[ccxliii] The Evansville Courier and Press, September 8, 1915, p. 8
[ccxliv] The Evansville Courier and Press, September 18, 1915. P. 3
[ccxlv] Ibid

[ccxlvi] Daily Republican-Register, October 16, 1915, p. 1
[ccxlvii] The Evansville Press, October 20, 1915, p. 1
[ccxlviii] Evansville Press, October 21, 1915, p. 1
[ccxlix] Ibid
[ccl] Ibid
[ccli] Ibid
[cclii] Ibid
[ccliii] Masked Marvel to the Rescue by author

www.ingramcontent.com/pod-product-compliance
Lightning Source LLC
LaVergne TN
LVHW010200070526
838199LV00062B/4439